Collins

KATHERINE MENGARDON

FOLLOW your DREAMS

100 INSPIRING AND EXTRAORDINARY JOBS

THE FUTURE iS NOW

Did you know that 85% of careers that will exist in 2030 haven't been invented yet?

THiNK ABOUT iT

Smart phones and social media are fairly recent inventions, taking off in 2007. YouTube started in 2005, and TikTok as recently as 2016...

And with each of these newcomers, a whole new set of skills and careers were born.

We live in a world where advances are faster than ever at all levels, led by technology, the environment, and the changing needs of our population.

ONLY 40 YEARS AgO

The world of work was completely transformed with the arrival of computers.

It made it possible for people to work together at speed and across continents in a way we couldn't have even dreamt of before. The COVID-19 pandemic also showed how fast we could adapt our work to a changing world. Working in an office is no longer always a necessity.

AND iT'S ABOUT TO HAPPEN AGAiN

In the next 15 years, experts predict that 40% of jobs will be done by AI, machine learning and robots.

We will always need teachers, doctors, lawyers, artists, designers, engineers, builders and more – but even these careers will be transformed in the future.

TiME TO FOLLOW YOUR DREAMS

This opens a world of opportunities to explore careers of the future in a different way – starting by giving what you love centre stage.

You might already know what you want to do when you grow up, or you may not have a clue. The chances are, your journey will take you through a few twists and turns.

WHAT YOU CARE ABOUT MATTERS

Each of us is a unique combination of things we love, things we are good at, and opportunities we encounter.

Do you love gaming, making videos, drawing manga? Or maybe you are really into caring for animals and nature? Do science, music, or fashion rock your world? Is your brain all about football, baking or coding?

WHATEVER iT iS

The reality is that each of these interests offers many brilliant and sometimes little-known career paths for you to explore, so here are 100 eye-popping and mind-sparking careers to get you started on your journey!

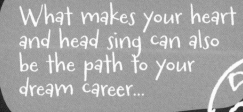

What makes your heart and head sing can also be the path to your dream career...

IF YOU adore ANIMALS...

Are you crushing on critters, fascinated by furry friends, a fan of all things feathery?

You might think the only careers out there are vet or zookeeper, but there are many other jobs in and around the animal world.

The best way to get started is to learn as much as you can about animals. Find out about their needs and habits by reading books, looking online or, better still, get experience in person.

Studying or working with wildlife generally happens in their natural environment – so if you like the outdoors, this could be perfect for you!

Be an alpaca farmer

FARMING CAN BE A WOOLLY BUSINESS

Do you love caring for animals and enjoy spending all your time outside, whatever the weather? Traditional farming is changing and there are plenty of options that could surprise you.

Straight from the South American mountains, alpacas are now becoming more common in farms across the world – not for their meat but for their wonderfully thick fleece! Alpaca wool is stronger, softer and warmer than sheep's wool, and is better for allergies. Their poo can even be turned into fuel, which is good news if you want your farm to be sustainable.

LLAMA TELL YOU ABOUT...

Alpacas (and their relatives, llamas) are very social and should be kept as a herd. Everyday care is at the heart of this job – so you'll need a proper routine to feed and keep your animals in good health. Their enclosure and shelter will also need to be well maintained. That aside, they are relatively easy to care for, as they don't need much space or grass to feed on.

DID YOU KNOW?

Alpacas and llamas may be quiet by nature, but they are very alert with strong eyesight. If they perceive any threat, they will scream really loudly! That's why many sheep farms in the UK use them as guardians for their flocks.

Be a primatologist

STUDY MONKEYS AND APES

Humans share over 90% of our DNA with primates, so it makes sense to pay attention to the biology and behaviour of our closest cousins. We can learn a lot about our past by observing how they socialise. It's also important to preserve their future as part of protecting our natural world.

BECOME A CHIMP CHAMPION

Primatologists can work in labs or in the wild – observing their daily habits, but also testing their reactions or diagnosing and treating animals. That means you might be away from home for long periods of time. You have to be prepared to rough it a bit – there might not always be a shower or a comfy bed around when you spend your days in the jungle!

MONKEY SEE, MONKEY DO

Primates are very social! If you do your job well and become part of their landscape, you might see them laugh, make jokes, groom each other – and don't expect them to respect your privacy either; they are curious creatures and you will become part of the troop.

WOULD YOU RATHER?

If working in the wild is not for you, you could work as a primate keeper in a zoo or sanctuary instead – you can stay close to home and still get plenty of ape action!

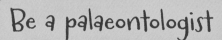

Be a palaeontologist

A NATURE DETECTIVE OF THE PAST

Did you know that an incredible 99% of all animals and plants that have ever existed on Earth are now extinct? And how do we know this, when there were no humans around to tell the tale? The answer: fossils! These are the preserved remains of animals and plants that lived on this planet millions of years ago, and a palaeontologist is someone who studies them.

By looking at fossilised animals and plants, as well as the landscapes they would have inhabited, palaeontologists can quite literally track the history of our planet and its ever-evolving biodiversity. It requires a good dose of curiosity and imagination, and a knack for science to make sure your findings are backed up with strong evidence.

FACING THE FUTURE

It might seem strange to bother about species that are no longer roaming the Earth, but with climate change, palaeontology is actually more relevant than ever. Scientists can use data from the distant past to predict how higher temperatures and carbon emissions will affect the planet in years to come.

FAIR-FEATHER FRIENDS

Did you know, it was by studying dinosaur fossils that palaeontologists discovered these creatures had feather-like features that related them to our present-day birds?

WOULD YOU RATHER?

There are many different branches to palaeontology – some scientists study microscopic organisms, while others specialise in coprolite (fossilised dinosaur poo!), which can tell us what they used to eat. Meanwhile, an ichnologist, another kind of palaeontologist, looks at the footprints and other traces left behind by long-extinct animals.

Be a wildlife photographer

CAPTURE BEAUTIFUL ANIMAL IMAGES

A wildlife photographer takes photos of animals in their natural habitat for books, magazines, and nature documentaries – but there's more to it than snapping pics! Patience is the name of the game here, as you might have to stake out your chosen animal for days, or even months! Being a keen nature-spotter is essential as you'll need to recognise signs of animal life, and understand how a particular species feeds, sleeps and plays so you can capture these moments on film.

GEAR UP!

You will need to have a keen interest in technology and an understanding of camera equipment to capture stunningly sharp images. Want to snap insects? Micro subjects require a macro lens that can capture tiny details. Want to catch a cheetah mid-chase in the savannah? You will need a camera set up that allows for catching superfast reactions. Batty for bats in the night sky? That lens will need to be capable of catching animal actions in very low light.

ONE IN A MILLION

When you see a stunning photograph of an eagle spreading its wings, it's easy to think the photographer just got lucky. But there's another secret: camera 'bursts' enable the photographer to take lots of pictures in the space of milliseconds – then they can simply choose the best one.

FIND YOUR FOCUS

Once back from the depths of the wild, another key part of the job will be to pick the best shots and 'edit' them to bring out depth, sharpness and colour, and create that perfect shot.

Meet real-life WILDLIFE PHOTOGRAPHER & FILM-MAKER Aishwarya Sridhar

WHY DID YOU CHOOSE YOUR JOB?

I grew up in the foothills of Matheran, near Mumbai city, so I had a strong bond with nature from childhood. But as I got older, I witnessed the devastating impact of human activity on our environment. Forests were being replaced by highways, and mangroves were being destroyed by polluting industries. It was then that I felt that I had to do something!

I began by advocating for conservation at local schools where I showcased the beauty of the lakes and forests, but also the way that trees were being cut down and how protecting the forests and wetland is vital for our survival. I used the images I had taken myself during my wildlife adventures in the school presentations.

Photographs and films showcasing pristine nature can make people fall in love with the wildlife and want to protect it, while hard-hitting stories of the issues plaguing our environment can shock people into action. By taking wildlife into the homes of people globally, I want them to know what can be lost, driving them to protect what's still left on our planet.

Aishwarya's photo of a tiger

HOW DID YOU GET INTO YOUR JOB?

My first attempt at wildlife film-making was born out of my relentless fight to save a wetland named Panje at Uran, close to my home. When the coastal city of Uran, in Maharashtra, India, was transformed from a birder's paradise into a concrete nightmare, Panje was the only wetland left. To protect it, I made a short film about it which was showcased on DD National (the Indian public service broadcaster). The film got a lot of appreciation and support from environmentalists and it encouraged me to take up filming environmental issues as a career that would bring about policy protection for wildlife globally.

Aishwarya ready to photograph wildlife

"Wildlife photography gives me a chance to be the voice for the voiceless."

WHAT QUALIFICATIONS AND EXPERIENCE DID YOU NEED TO DO THE JOB?

I studied mass media which certainly helped me be a better storyteller, but I didn't formally learn film-making. Whatever knowledge I have, I have learnt on the job. But to be a great wildlife storyteller, you need to have an eye for detail, knowledge of your camera and loads of patience... sometimes you have to wait for days at a spot in order to get the shot you want!

WHAT ARE THE HIGHLIGHTS OF YOUR JOB?

One highlight is that wildlife photography and film-making gives me a chance to be the voice for the voiceless. My work has also taken me on thrilling adventures, from being up close and personal with super-cool creatures, to covering some of the most dangerous wildlife black markets in Asia.

A bonnet macaque by Aishwarya

11

Be an insect taxonomist

A SCIENTIST WHO SORTS AND NAMES INSECTS

Insect taxonomists are scientists who identify bugs and group them into categories. They have closely studied one million species so far, painstakingly classifying and naming each one. But there are still a whopping estimated 10 million more to go, so we need a lot more taxonomists to identify them before they're gone!

WORM YOUR WAY IN

If worms and woodlice rock your world, taxonomy is a brilliant career to consider. Insects are found on all seven continents (even Antarctica has insects, if very few), so you might get to travel, help develop insect-friendly products for use in gardens and homes, and who knows, maybe even have a species named after you.

WHAT'S THE BUZZ?

They may be tiny, but insects alone account for over half of all animal life on Earth and play a crucial role: most fruits, vegetables, honey and even chocolate would disappear without our pollinating creepy crawlies. They are an essential snack staple for many birds, amphibians and mammals. Yet insects are disappearing faster than ever, causing a real threat to our world. This is why understanding bugs of all kinds, and their role in our ecosystem, is more important than ever.

REUSE, RECYCLE, RECREATE

If you ever needed more proof that we really are dependent on insects, think about this: when animals and plants die, it is insects that break them down and recycle them back into our ecosystem. The world would be overwhelmed with dead things without them!

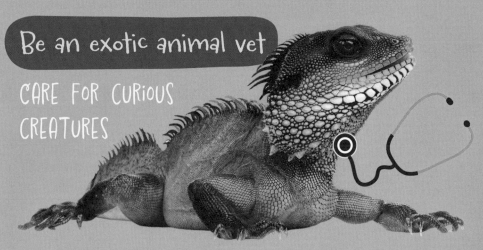

Be an exotic animal vet

CARE FOR CURIOUS CREATURES

When we think of vets, we generally think of a cat or dog doctor – but what do you do when your pet of choice is a snake, a parrot, or a bearded dragon? When they need medical care, you call an exotic animal vet!

FANTASTIC BEASTS

These vets are highly specialised, treating birds, reptiles and unusual mammals that have very different needs to more common household pets. But they don't just work with family pets; in this role you might also be called to care for animals in zoos or in wildlife centres, or you might work in a dedicated exotic animal clinic. Your day might include treating anything from a huge elephant to a tiny capuchin monkey!

PECULIAR PROBLEMS

In this job, it's likely no two days will ever be the same. One day in a vet practice your patients might include a troubled tortoise or a chilly chinchilla; the next you might need to use your expertise to tend to a badly behaved budgie in a rescue centre!

SNAKES AND JOB LADDERS

You will need to start by becoming a qualified veterinarian, then take extra courses to learn how to care for more unusual species. The type of animals you decide to include in your training is up to you, but whatever you do, you will need to be able to think quickly on your feet to solve what might be wrong with an animal, and leave any squeamish fear behind as dealing with pus, blood and poo will all be part of your job!

Be a cat behaviourist

HELP CAT OWNERS UNDERSTAND THEIR FELINE FRIENDS

If the sheer number of cat videos on the internet is anything to go by, people are more fond of felines than ever before – yet our furry friends can be hard to read. Just like humans, cats display their emotions through behaviour that can sometimes be rather puzzling. Why is your cat scratching that chair? Or peeing on the carpet? Is your cat anxious when you leave the room? And what exactly are they meowing about? Call the cat behaviourist!

WHAT'S UP PUSSYCAT?

As the name suggests, a cat behaviourist works with the owner to examine the cat's behaviour: their daily habits, any changes in their environment, and their interactions with humans or other animals. They might visit the home, or consult online through video calls, photos and by requesting information from the owner. They might consult vets too to check if a particular behaviour might have a medical cause.

CAT SCAN

Once they have a proper view of the situation, they will write a report to suggest how to train away any behaviour issues, along with advice on how the owner can make sure their cat is as happy as can be.

THE PURRFECT JOB

If spending every day thinking like a cat makes you purr with joy, training as a behaviourist could be your dream job!

Be an equine therapist

USE THE HEALING POWER OF HORSES

Sometimes it's animals that can teach us a thing or two about our own behaviour. Equine (horse) therapy is just that. Working as a team, a professional therapist and a horse handler help people overcome issues – anything from dealing with anxiety to recovering from the trauma of an accident or difficult life experiences.

GIDDY UP!

During sessions, a therapist might help the patient do very simple things, like grooming, feeding, or leading a horse. Horses don't use words, of course, so equine therapists have to understand their body language. This can often help us understand our own feelings and needs as we learn to recognise these cues.

If being the horse handler appeals to you more, you will be the expert that ensures everyone is safe – horse and human alike. You will have a close relationship with the horse, caring for them daily, knowing their personality, and training them.

STABLE MATE

Your work day will likely be spent mostly in stables and paddocks, but you might also take your horse on visits to care homes, for example, where people who can't come to you can benefit from the calming presence of horses.

GENTLE GIANTS

Did you know, many horses are gentle and calm by nature? They might look big and imposing, but they are very social creatures, and can pick up and respond to human emotions.

Be a marine biologist

STUDY LIFE UNDER THE SEA

Do you sometimes think what fun it would be to have gills instead of lungs? To be able to breathe and swim under water with the fishes? If so, a sub-aquatic life could be for you.

As a scientist who studies animals and plants that live in the ocean, you would be helping to understand the marine world better while investigating the impact of human activity on ocean life – by collecting and analysing samples and observing and recording changes over time. You might also be required to create maps and set up experiments.

WAVE YOURSELF IN

You will need to be patient, curious, methodical and keen to figure out and explain your findings. Work takes place in laboratories and offices, but you would also spend a lot of time studying animals and plants in their natural environment. That means plenty of boat trips and diving, and you will need to become a strong swimmer too.

TAKE THE PLUNGE

To get you started, watching nature documentaries can give you incredible insights into sea creatures. And if you find yourself on a beach or visiting an aquarium, do make the most of it and get observing!

DID YOU KNOW?

Up to 80% of life on Earth is found in the oceans. And we've only explored a fraction of it, so budding marine biologists have still got plenty more to discover.

Be a service dog trainer

TRAIN PUPPIES TO BECOME SKILLED HELPERS

Would you describe yourself as energetic, sociable, always up for a run and wanting to play – some might say a bit puppy-like? Then you might want to consider a career in training service dogs. It's not just about playing with puppies though, but also teaching important skills, which requires some serious patience, gentleness and consistency.

BARKING UP THE RIGHT TREE

A service dog trainer will start working with puppies by socialising them from an early age, and teaching them to assist people who have different physical or mental health needs. Dogs are known as a human's best friend, and it's never more true than with a service dog.

SPECIAL SKILLS

Service dogs can learn to detect early signs of seizures or emotional distress in their owners and will help to keep them safe, either through their companionship or by bringing them essential medicine. Having a four-legged companion by their side can give a new lease of independence to people who are blind, deaf or have mobility issues.

GIVE YOURSELF A ROUND OF A PAWS!

Service dogs are trained for very specific conditions and trainers use their expertise to match the right dog to the right owner, as they will need to form a very close bond. Did you know, Labradors and German Shepherds respond particularly well to training, and are often chosen for the trickiest of tasks?

IF YOUR *heart* SAYS art...

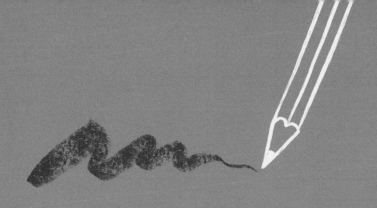

A simple pencil sketch holds the power to unleash our wildest imaginings, without limits. Do you find yourself captivated by drawing or painting – endlessly creating lines, shapes, shadows and colours? A wide range of careers is out there to spark your artistic talents, offering a rich palette of opportunities.

Imaginary characters and stories can be developed through design, and illustration can be used to plan something unique and beautiful. Whether sketching on paper or exploring digital realms, drawing leads you down career avenues that will stretch your abilities, while the strokes of your pencil or stylus will leave an everlasting impression, way beyond the limits of your work desk.

Be a mural artist

BRING ART TO THE STREETS

Not long ago, almost all street murals – that's art painted on an outside wall – were seen as rebellious graffiti, frowned upon by society. But today, they are often celebrated as real art, bringing life and colour to our cities. This remarkable change has given mural artists a chance to express themselves in powerful ways away from traditional art galleries. The modern street artist must, of course, make sure they have the necessary permission from the local council or property owner – but once they have this, they can let their imagination lead the way! And the great thing is, street artists will be paid for their artistry.

BIG PICTURE

With the freedom to work on a big scale, mural artists leave their mark on communities. You will get to work with local governments, businesses, and art groups to transform dull urban walls. Your captivating masterpieces will leave passers-by uplifted and inspired.

THE WORLD IS YOUR CANVAS

A day in the life of a mural artist is full of creativity. First you must plan your project with smaller-scale sketches on a computer or on paper. Then when it's time to get to the painting itself, there will be long, intensive hours spent outdoors to bring your vision to reality.

ARTING AROUND

Becoming a mural artist requires a mix of traditional and modern techniques. You will need to know how to use colours effectively and mastering spray paint is essential for creating large-scale murals. And don't forget, mural artists use scaffolding platforms to access the outside of high buildings – so anyone with a fear of heights should stay at ground level!

Be a courtroom sketcher

DRAW COURT SCENES FROM MEMORY

If you want to add a bit of drama to your artistic career, courtroom sketching might be just the right canvas for your talents. The job of a courtroom sketcher is to draw illustrations of the key people involved in a trial, to be used in the news.

EYES OF THE LAW

This traditional work remains relevant even in our tech-savvy age. Cameras are usually not allowed in the courtroom. Equally, drawing during legal proceedings is forbidden – so you, the sketcher, have to be able to draw from memory after the hearing is over. You become the visual connection, offering an insight to the media and the public, helping everyone better understand the unfolding of a criminal trial and communicating its particular mood and atmosphere.

SPEED DRAWING

To flourish in this career, you'll need to be able to work fast and accurately and have a talent for conveying human emotions through your art. Courtroom artists tend to use charcoal pencils and pastels as these allow them to draw and build colour quickly.

FIRST-HAND WITNESS

You will get to watch high-profile criminal cases first hand, and you will need to respect the confidentiality and formality of the trial while it's taking place. It's common for courtroom artists to leave the faces of jurors and vulnerable witnesses blank to protect their privacy.

Be a restoration artist

BRiNG ANCiENT ART BACK TO LiFE

Imagine a job where your canvas isn't a blank piece of paper, but a piece of history, weathered by time. That's what it's like to be a restoration artist. They restore, repair, and preserve works of art – protecting our cultural heritage so future generations get to enjoy beautiful creations from the past. The role of a restoration artist is not just about conservation; it's about keeping our stories alive and ensuring that history never fades.

THE FiNER DETAiLS

First things first, you'll need to channel your inner artist. Drawing and painting skills will be your bread and butter, as you'll be recreating the past – brushstroke by brushstroke. You'll also need good attention to detail to identify the materials used in pieces of artwork, then match those materials exactly and restore these treasures in a way that is authentic to the time period.

PATiENCE iS A ViRTUE

Restoration is a slow process, so you'll need patience as you painstakingly piece history back together. And, of course, a love of history and culture is a must! A background in art history or conservation is typically where you start – but it's not all learning from books. Practical art experience through internships or apprenticeships will be the key to practising your craft.

MASTER OF MASTERPiECES

Restoration artists can work in all sorts of places, from churches to museums and even in their own studios. Whatever the workplace, you'll be in a controlled environment, carefully preserving the past for the benefit of the future. There will be some pressure, as you'll be entrusted with irreplaceable masterpieces, but the satisfaction of bringing history back to life is unparalleled. It's like being a creative time-traveller repairing art's time-worn wrinkles!

Be a medical illustrator

LIKE A DOCTOR OF DRAWING!

Medical illustration is where creativity and medical knowledge meet to bring science to life through art. In their daily work, medical illustrators use their artistic skills to create accurate and engaging illustrations of the human body. Their work might appear in textbooks, scientific journals, digital animations, and material given to patients to help them better understand their health – making medical information accessible to everyone.

CALL THE DOCTOR

It's essential to understand what you want to explain, so you would have to work closely with doctors, surgeons, nurses and patients to capture all of the information you need to create the best possible images. You're likely to spend quite a bit of time in hospitals or in university medical departments.

BLENDING TECHNIQUES

A remarkable aspect of this field is how it brings together traditional art and modern technology. Some illustrators might draw by hand using pens, ink or paints, while others will use advanced digital tools to create 3D models and animations. Photography is another key tool of the trade to record findings before turning them into illustrations.

PAPYRUS TRAIL

Did you know that medical illustration has a long history, dating back to ancient Egypt? They recorded surgical procedures and anatomy on papyrus scrolls, laying the groundwork for this modern career.

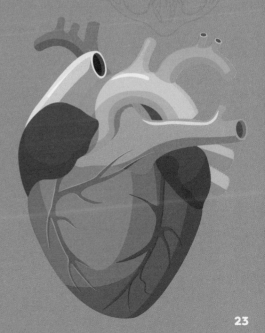

Be a digital retoucher

MAKE PHOTOS LOOK PICTURE PERFECT

Are you determined to make your photos pop? Do you love playing with colours and filters to make them look the best they can? Digital retouching is the process of editing and enhancing photographic images using software to improve their appearance or correct imperfections. This can include layering and combining visual elements, correcting colour to help you achieve the right light levels and mood (known as colour grading), and adding visual effects. By mastering these techniques, you'll soon be turning ordinary photographs into extraordinary masterpieces.

VISUAL STORYTELLING

This is a job that can lead you to work in all sorts of industries – from fashion to advertising, entertainment to e-commerce (online sales). Businesses and creative people alike need digital retouching experts to add that extra spark to their images for online content, magazines, catalogues, adverts and more.

TRAINED EYE

Armed with cutting-edge software and artistic flair, you'll get to use the latest techniques to improve images. You don't need lots of academic qualifications to become a digital retoucher, but having a portfolio showcasing your best work is a must. Some formal training in graphic design or photography is an advantage, but a keen eye for detail and the ability to learn and grow on the job will also get you places.

Be a tattoo artist

THE HUMAN BODY IS YOUR CANVAS

There is no end to artistic expression when it comes to tattoos – some people will be after something realistic, while others might want something more fantastical. Some will want something discreet, while others may want to use their entire body as a canvas.

To be a tattoo artist, you will have to learn to work meticulously, understand the best places to ink a specific tattoo on the body, and how human skin holds tattoo ink. Mastering proper hygiene practices is also very important. Eco-friendly and vegan inks are gaining popularity, so you'll need to know all the options to give your clients what they want.

NOW YOU SEE ME, NOW YOU DON'T

It might surprise you to learn that part of a tattoo artist's job is to remove tattoos using special lasers. They can also refresh or modify fading tattoos and make them look as good as new. Some tattoo artists may even use special ink that reacts to light, creating tattoos that are invisible in regular light but glow under ultraviolet light.

NEEDLING ACROSS TIME

Did you know, tattoos held symbolic meanings in many ancient cultures? For centuries, the Māori people of New Zealand have inked distinct facial tattoos called tā moko; these are unique to each individual, representing their ancestry and life story.

Be a jewellery maker

CREATE NECKLACES, BRACELETS, RINGS, AND OTHER SHINY THINGS

If you find yourself drawn to shiny gems – and drawn to drawing them! – a career as a jewellery maker might be the perfect fit for you. Throughout history, jewellery has been seen as a symbol of wealth and status, a token of love, and an opportunity for personal expression. Today it's an industry that continues to flourish, both for the artisan jewellery maker who crafts one-of-a-kind pieces by hand, and for the designers who work for large retailers to create the latest jewellery lines.

SPARKLE AND SHINE

Day to day, jewellery makers sketch their creations before transforming raw precious metals and gemstones into wearable works of art. As with any craft, jewellery making demands dedication and patience – you will need to learn the best techniques to melt, mould and work with gold, silver and other metals, as well as how to cut and polish stones to a glittering finish.

ONE OF A KIND

Jewellery makers can sometimes be involved in designing a unique piece for a very special moment or milestone in someone's life, like an engagement, a wedding, or an anniversary. Occasionally, you might be asked to repurpose an older piece, giving it a new lease of life.

THE FUTURE IS BRIGHT

Technological advancements, like 3D printing and new ways to work with unusual raw materials like resin, wood, plastic or even concrete, are offering fresh avenues for experimentation and giving the jewellery makers of tomorrow lots to look forward to!

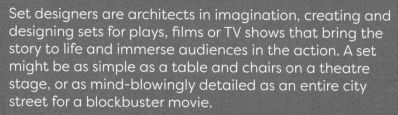

CREATE PROPS AND BACKDROPS FOR FILM, TV AND THEATRE

Set designers are architects in imagination, creating and designing sets for plays, films or TV shows that bring the story to life and immerse audiences in the action. A set might be as simple as a table and chairs on a theatre stage, or as mind-blowingly detailed as an entire city street for a blockbuster movie.

As a set designer, you'll be an essential part of the artistic team, collaborating with directors, lighting designers, and costume artists to craft the stage or set. Your keen eye for detail, and ability to imagine spaces, will transport audiences to new worlds and transform blank stages and screens into vivid, convincing displays.

EVER-CHANGING SCENE

No two sets are the same! One day, you might be crafting a realistic backdrop like a simple living-room for a sitcom; the next, you'll find yourself designing a fantastical world filled with futuristic props for a film. And best of all, each time, you'll get to experience the joy of witnessing actors work within the spaces you've created.

PRACTICALLY MINDED

Set design isn't just about creativity; it also demands meticulous planning and problem-solving. You'll start by putting pencil to paper to draft your designs, or creating 3D models by using software and projection mapping (a way to project images or videos onto objects or surfaces to create 3D effects).

You will need to consider stage or set dimensions and possible locations, as well as the practicalities of scene changes – balancing the actors' needs and the director's vision.

TURN DELICIOUS CAKES INTO MASTERPIECES

Do you have a serious sweet tooth? Are you always dreaming up delicious desserts and creamy confections? Hold onto your oven mitts then, because a career as a cake decorator might be for you!

Culinary decorating has long been used as a way to turn ordinary food into edible works of art. By playing with different frostings and exciting toppings, anything from humble cupcakes to three-tier sponge cakes can be turned into jaw-dropping masterpieces. Your job will often involve responding to client requests for one-of-a-kind designs for special occasions, like weddings and birthday parties, and your decorated cake creations will leave your clients amazed and make their taste buds dance with joy.

SWEET STUFF!

The perks of being a cake decorator are as sweet as your creations. Working for a bakery, café, restaurant, hotel or catering company, or starting your very own company, you will get to explore traditional and new baking techniques, experiment with unusual flavour combinations, and take pride in bringing happiness to others through your art. Plus, you'll be surrounded by the mouth-watering aroma of fresh baking every working day – truly the icing on the cake!

BAKE IT TO THE LIMIT

Fun fact – around 250 bakers and cake decorators broke the Guinness World Record in 2015 for the largest cake sculpture ever made: a 244-square-metre creation in the shape of Italy, complete with famous landmarks made of icing sugar, buttercream beaches, sponge mountains, and miniature houses and boats! It took four days to assemble, weighed 1,000 kg and fed 12,000 people.

Be a comic book creator

DEVELOP AND DRAW COMIC STRIPS

Unless you have been living in a galaxy far, far away, you will have seen comic book stories taking over our screens, big and small – and manga, anime and graphic novels of all kinds are also on the rise. Comic book creators write these stories and illustrate them with hand-drawn, cartoon-style illustrations.

JACK OR JILL OF ALL TRADES

Comic book creators are not only fantastic at drawing, but also accomplished scriptwriters and designers who can translate a story visually on the page. When working for big comics, they might take a more specialised role depending on their specific skills, working with top talent across the industry as illustrators, pencillers, writers, inkers, colourers or letterers (more careers right there to explore!).

FREEDOM OF EXPRESSION

But even with all that collaboration, it's a job that requires you to be happy to work on your own. Drawing can be done anywhere and at any time; as long as you deliver the work on time. So it's the sort of career that gives you a lot of freedom to work and live as you please.

EMBRACE THE METAVERSE

Ask anyone working in the creation of comic books and, chances are, they started out very young by copying drawings of, and writing stories about, their favourite characters – and they've never stopped! The best way to make it in this industry is to just draw and write, then draw and write some more!

Meet real-life
COMIC ILLUSTRATOR
Mike Collins

WHY DID YOU CHOOSE TO DO YOUR JOB?

When I was two years old, I discovered comics and it made me start drawing. At age three, I decided that's what I wanted to do when I grew up. And I did!

HOW DID YOU GET INTO IT?

It wasn't always easy. At first, I would spend hours tracing characters I liked but little by little I grew more confident and developed my own style. The best way to learn is actually to draw, draw and draw some more. I was told time and time again that illustrating comics wasn't a real job, so I went to university to study Law. While I was at university, I spent a couple of years getting my work known at Marvel UK by sending in drawings, before eventually they gave me my first paid job. I thought I would become known as the Barrister that draws Spider-Man – but I soon realised I was much better at comics, so I dropped the wig for a pencil once and for all. I haven't stopped working since, and have drawn pretty much any superhero you can think of!

"The best way to learn is actually to draw, draw and draw some more!"

WHAT'S iT LiKE iLLUSTRATiNG COMICS?

I work from home mostly, but I do get to travel the world for events like Comic Cons. That's how I saw Stan Lee a few times. He is the creator of Spider-Man and my personal hero, but I never dared introduce myself. I met Jack Kirby though, who drew many of the first Marvel Comics (Thor, Iron Man, The Fantastic Four, The Avengers).

I never thought I would do anything else but draw comics, but I also create storyboards for films and TV, like Horrid Henry, Doctor Who and Sherlock Holmes. And if you have any merchandise from these shows, like T-shirts or mugs, chances are you are wearing my work! I was amazed when I saw Sheldon in The Big Bang Theory carrying a Doctor Who lunch box I'd designed!

Even when I'm on holiday, I draw. It's what I do, and I'm so lucky that my job is also what I love doing best.

Top tip: use as few lines as possible when drawing faces – more lines makes them look older!

Mike concentrating on the illustrations for a comic

31

f

%

IF YOU'RE A

maths marvel...

μ

+

X

fx-83GT X

CLASSWIZ

You can count on numbers and statistics to deliver some surprising career options. Though you might assume that totting up figures only has a few everyday uses, that would be missing the mark. Mathematicians are tasked with solving big problems, recognising patterns in large amounts of data, and explaining how things work in a logical way. Their work applies to most areas of our lives.

Working with numbers often requires lots of studying, number crunching, dealing with complex spreadsheets, and working in an office environment. But real-world observation is bound to play a part too, and this can take you to some interesting places – adding up to a rich and exciting working life.

Be a meteorologist

EXPLORE PATTERNS TO PREDICT THE WEATHER

Have you ever wondered where the weather forecast comes from? The job of a meteorologist is to study the weather, collecting an enormous amount of data from the land, sea, and atmosphere (the gases surrounding our planet) to understand weather patterns and make accurate predictions. Meteorology impacts many aspects of our lives: it helps us to plan outdoor adventures, stay dry on rainy days, and stay safe from storms.

BREEZY DOES IT

For a job that relies so much on what's happening in the sky above our heads, most of a meteorologist's time is spent indoors analysing information on a computer screen. Every day, they access a number of different measuring instruments located all across the world, like radar and satellite images, to predict how the weather will change over time. They use mathematics to analyse patterns and test different scenarios, figuring out the most likely weather outcomes for their forecast.

TRULY ENLIGHTENING

But meteorology doesn't just tell us whether or not we are going to need an umbrella tomorrow. It supports many other important industries. Farmers rely on weather predictions to grow healthy crops, while airlines and shipping businesses use meteorological information to ensure safe travel. Energy companies also depend on weather forecasts to harness the power of wind and sun to generate eco-friendly energy, helping us work towards a greener future.

MOMENT IN THE SUN

Talking about the weather is one of the most common conversations we have in our daily lives. So, if you're mathematically minded and fancy spending your time figuring out what Mother Nature has in store for us, your work could be the talk of the town.

Be an urban planner

SHAPE THE FUTURE OF OUR CITIES

The cities, towns, and villages that we live in are ever-changing. As their populations grow, so do their needs – and this is where urban planners come in. Just like in many simulation games, it's crucial to have people who plan the development and future of our communities, considering lots of complex factors like housing, industry, agriculture, transport, recreation, and the environment. Their aim is to create attractive, accessible, and eco-friendly spaces where residents can live, work, and play.

CITY LIMITS

As an urban planner, you will visit and research the area, analyse data sets, keep up with legislation on how land can be used, and develop planning proposals for how the town or city will run. Much of your work will be done on computers, using maps, satellite images, surveys and databases to paint a picture of the urban landscape. From designing pedestrian-friendly neighbourhoods to ensuring that green spaces are not overwhelmed by too many houses or roads, the decisions you make will have a profound impact on people's lives.

PLANNING POWER

The positive influence of urban planning extends to lots of different industries. It guides the construction of transportation systems, ensuring smooth commutes and reducing congestion. It creates educational and healthcare facilities, encouraging vibrant and healthy communities. Urban planning even plays a role in economic development by attracting businesses to town – so by doing your dream job, you'll also be creating job opportunities for others!

GiVE LiFE TO CHARACTERS AND STORiES ON SCREEN

Animations, like cartoons and animated films, allow us to experience imaginary worlds that are brought to life not by actors, but by drawings, models, and computers. An animator makes these animations, producing multiple images called 'frames' that create an illusion of movement when watched together. This might sound like a very arty career – and it is – but maths and numbers play a crucial role too. Animators have to use formulas and algorithms (sets of mathematical instructions) to create 3D models and figure out how to make their animations look realistic.

STEP BY STEP

Animators use computer programs to figure out how a character will move naturally and convincingly. They have to consider how long their walking stride might be, and how their character's height, weight or situation would affect this. An elegant giraffe, for example, will move very differently to a cheeky mouse scuttling away with a piece of cheese it just stole! Animators will experiment on their characters by applying mathematical principles found in physics – acceleration, pressure, mass, and friction – until every step is flawless.

MOVE FORWARD

Animators are hired to work for production companies, animation studios, and computer game developers. They usually collaborate with a wider creative team, combining artistic talents and numeracy skills to create beautiful, believable animations. You will need to learn basic animation skills like timing, movement, and character design to create life-like animations that transport audiences to magical worlds. The best way to start is by playing with free online animation software. Plenty of animators are self-taught, or start with college or university courses.

TURN NUMBERS INTO SPORTING STRATEGY

If you add passion for sports to a love of crunching numbers, your dream job just might equal sports statistician. These are data scientists who specialise in the world of sports. They meticulously measure, record, and analyse data about movement, fitness, nutrition and performance across sporting events and training, using statistical analysis to uncover meaningful insights and trends. Their findings are used by coaches to evaluate players and improve individual and team performances.

EXERCISE YOUR BRAIN

Watch any sport on TV and you'll see commentators relying on stats and trends that are established by sports statisticians. To succeed in the job, you will need to understand every aspect of the sport – from the physical fitness of athletes, their performance in previous games, and how different terrains or weather might affect play. Knowing the numbers is only part of the job; it takes someone with a deep understanding and attention to detail to be a game-changer.

STROKE OF GENIUS

When world records, medals and trophies are at stake, any insight has the power to turn sport performance from great to truly outstanding. Statisticians work with professional athletes, sports teams, leagues, broadcasters and more. This is a career where your mathematical skills would be at the heart of shaping the future of sports, enhancing the overall sporting experience for players, coaches and the audience itself.

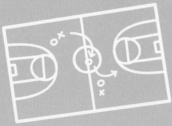

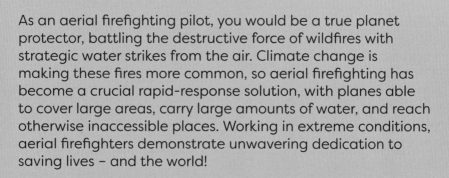

Be an aerial firefighting pilot

PUT OUT FIRES BY PLANE

As an aerial firefighting pilot, you would be a true planet protector, battling the destructive force of wildfires with strategic water strikes from the air. Climate change is making these fires more common, so aerial firefighting has become a crucial rapid-response solution, with planes able to cover large areas, carry large amounts of water, and reach otherwise inaccessible places. Working in extreme conditions, aerial firefighters demonstrate unwavering dedication to saving lives – and the world!

BLAZE OF GLORY

You will, of course, need specialist training and exceptional flying skills (many aerial firefighters are trained first as commercial or military pilots), plus quick decision making and a good dose of courage. You'll have to navigate through turbulent air currents and dense smoke, all while ensuring the safety of everyone onboard. Imagine the adrenaline rush of flying over fierce flames, executing precise manoeuvres to release thousands of gallons of water to contain the fire. It's as heroic a job as it gets – but what does it have to do with maths?

FLIGHT FACTORS

The reason you need to know your numbers for this career is that mission success relies on you and your team working out in advance very precise calculations around fuel consumption, the weight of the water, and estimated flight time. Working with numbers is equally important during the actual operation. From the air, pilots calculate the exact amount of fire-retardant or water to drop based on the intensity, location, and trajectory of the fire (where it's heading next). They must also assess weather patterns and determine the direction of the wind, adjusting their flight path accordingly.

UNCOVER THE MYSTERIES OF THE UNIVERSE

Astronomers are explorers of the universe! They observe and analyse celestial objects like planets, stars, galaxies, and black holes. Equipped with deep-space passion and a thirst for cosmic knowledge, astronomers dedicate their careers to understanding what goes on beyond our world.

ASTRO-ALGORITHMS

Astronomers use powerful telescopes and cutting-edge technology to collect data about space and work towards Earth-shattering discoveries. They apply mathematical principles in their work to calculate the routes of satellites and rockets, estimate the position of distant stars and galleries, and formulate theories about the universe. They also use mathematical models to predict celestial events, like meteor showers, eclipses, and supermoons (this is when the moon is full and at its closest point to Earth, making it look big and bright!).

OVER THE MOON

By pursuing a career in astronomy, you'll be blasting off on a lifelong journey of research and exploration, working in laboratories for either universities, government agencies, observatories or private space-related companies – pushing the boundaries of human knowledge far beyond the edge of the Earth. You'll need a strong background in maths and physics, an analytical mind for solving problems with logic, as well as top-notch computer skills.

SHOOT FOR THE STARS

Astronomers have recently played a pivotal role in unveiling the existence of exoplanets – planets that orbit a star outside our solar system. This is one of the most significant discoveries in our understanding of the cosmos as it makes us reconsider some of the biggest questions about space. Are we alone in the universe? What makes a planet habitable? How do planets come to exist? Clearly there is still plenty left to explore for astronomers, present and future!

Be a composer

USE MATHS TO CREATE MUSIC

With a deep understanding of musical theory, a keen ear for harmony, and an incredible imagination, a composer writes original music that tells stories, evokes emotions, and resonates with audiences. But did you know, composers are often skilled mathematicians too?

NO MINOR FEAT

At its core, music is a mathematical language – rhythm, harmony, and melody are structured through numerical relationships and patterns. Composers use ratios, proportions, and intervals to make music sound good. They also use things like notes and beats on paper to talk to other musicians.

MATHEMATICAL MELODIES

So, if you want to be a composer, being good at maths can be really helpful. For example, when you write music, you might use fractions to show how long a note should be, like making a half note last twice as long as a quarter note. This helps musicians play the music just right.

TUNE INTO TECH

Today, composers often use maths and computer tools to help them create new musical ideas and try different methods of making music. Technology helps them understand the structure of music better, change sounds, and create intricate pieces. Composers can work for themselves or for music companies, and they can create music for various genres like classical, pop, electronic, and more. They might work in studios, concert halls, or even simply from home with their computers.

Be an AI programmer

USE THE POWER OF ARTIFICIAL INTELLIGENCE

Artificial intelligence, or AI, is when computers are able to think and learn, so they can perform tasks that are usually done by people. Have you ever used a chatbot on a website? An AI programmer will have created the code that enables the programme to recognise what you ask and how to best respond. AI is transforming the way we live and work by collecting information or data to do things automatically that might take a person hours to do, creating personalised recommendations and making decisions. As AI technology continues to evolve, the demand for AI jobs will grow too – in this sector, business is booming!

CODING RULES

Skills like critical thinking and creative problem-solving are essential. A programmer writing code for AI will need to use mathematics, statistics and calculus rules to teach AI systems to recognise things they have to respond to, like pictures or specific words, so they can give the best suggestions.

SMART TECHNOLOGY

Working with AI involves a deep understanding of computers and coding. So it's no surprise that many AI experts have backgrounds in video games, because these games use advanced AI techniques to create lifelike characters, strategic opponents and immersive experiences. So, if you're a passionate gamer who spends a lot of time online, you might find your gaming skills come in very handy for a career in AI.

WOULD YOU RATHER?

Technology is entwined in every aspect of our lives. That means someone with AI programming skills has the option to work across pretty much any industry: healthcare, finance, cybersecurity, manufacturing – the list goes on and on!

Be an extreme architect

PLAN EXTRAORDINARY STRUCTURES

Extreme architecture is a way to respond to the needs of our growing population and the challenges of climate change. Imagine being the mastermind behind buildings that harness harsh winds or collect water from the depths of the ground in an arid desert. This is the world of extreme architects – daring visionaries who meld art, science and creativity to create the city landscapes of tomorrow.

Extreme architects are meticulous problem-solvers. They have to wrestle with many challenges to develop structures that are both stable and environmentally friendly. It's a balancing act between beauty, safety and functionality. They are not afraid to dream big and can turn their ideas into reality thanks to their understanding of mathematics and engineering.

IMAGINE THIS

If you find yourself constantly dreaming up extraordinary structures, this could be a fantastic career path for you. You will need a strong foundation in architecture, through a degree but also through hands-on experience – during internships or apprenticeships – to develop your craft.

HOME ICY HOME

Located in one of the northernmost lands in the world, the Snowhotel in Norway is a structure made entirely of ice and snow. It embraces the extreme cold temperatures, revisiting traditional building techniques to welcome visitors who want to enjoy this unique winter environment.

PEAK BUILD

The Messner Mountain Museum in Italy (pictured above) is perched on top of Mount Kronplatz in the Alps. This futuristic structure takes inspiration from, and blends in with, the surrounding peaks to offer spectacular views. It was designed by renowned visionary architect Zaha Hadid, who is recognised as a pioneer in extreme architecture. Many of her buildings are now important landmarks in major cities.

DESIGN RIDES FOR THRILL-SEEKERS

Life is full of ups and downs – especially if you design rollercoasters for a living! A rollercoaster engineer is someone who dreams up, builds, and maintains all types of amusement park rides, everything from hair-raising rollercoasters to cute carousels. They combine the technical skill of an engineer with the creativity of a designer, making rides that put the FUN in functional!

IN FOR A WILD RIDE

All engineers need a strong foundation in maths and physics – you will need to understand the concepts of force, gravity, motion, momentum, and structural integrity. An eye for detail and strong problem-solving skills are also essential for spotting potential design flaws and coming up with innovative solutions. After finalising the blueprints (the technical drawings of the rides), rollercoaster engineers will oversee construction crews and work closely with technicians – watching their designs come to life and keeping the rides running smoothly.

SAFELY SCARY

Most importantly of all, rollercoaster engineers are responsible for creating and implementing safety features on their rides. This presents a unique challenge – to create the impression of danger, while keeping riders safe from start to finish.

QUEUE JUMPER

As a rollercoaster engineer, one of the perks of the job is being first in line to test out your creations – after those important safety checks, but before they open to the general public!

Meet real-life THRILL ENGINEER Brendan Walker

WHAT iS YOUR JOB?

I specialise in understanding how and why people feel different emotions – like fear, happiness, and especially thrill! I then design and engineer amusement rides and attraction experiences to make people feel these emotions. I've worked on rollercoasters, but right now I'm focusing on using virtual reality to make the experience of simple playground swings feel a hundred times more thrilling. That's why I call myself a Thrill Engineer!

HOW DiD YOU GET iNTO THE JOB?

I studied aeronautical engineering at Imperial College, then trained at British Aerospace and worked on jet aircraft. But that wasn't exciting enough... I wanted to invent and create new things! So, I left to study Industrial Design at the Royal College of Art.

When I left art college I worked for small design studios, designing everything from toys for pet ferrets, to stage microphones for popstars. I was once asked to design interactive exhibits for London's Science Museum. That's when I really started to get interested in thrill! I started to experiment and build my own machines in my workshop and give talks about my work.

"The job of Thrill Engineer didn't exist – I had to invent it!"

Rollercoaster Oblivion at Alton Towers

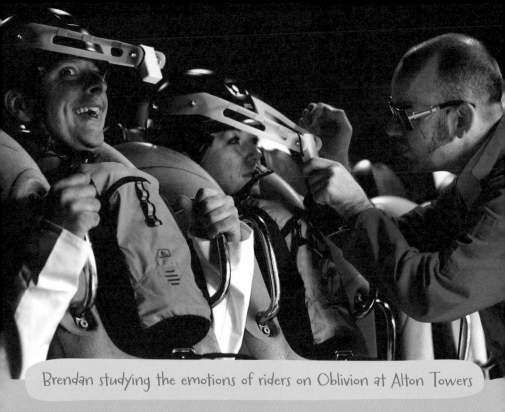

Brendan studying the emotions of riders on Oblivion at Alton Towers

Years later, the museum invited me back to organise an exhibition and series of events called Thrill Laboratory (now the name of my company). I brought different fairground rides into the museum, and used them to talk about lots of topics, including physics, psychology and biology. I invented 'Thrill Engineer' as a character to help me communicate my ideas. The job of Thrill Engineer didn't exist – I had to invent it!

AND WHAT ARE THE BEST BITS ABOUT YOUR JOB?

The most exciting thing about performing Thrill Laboratory at the Science Museum was that the owners of Thorpe Park and Alton Towers saw what I was doing and asked me to help study and design new rides for them!

IF YOU'RE A
PLANET PROTECTOR...

If you're fuelled by a deep love for nature and a burning desire to make a difference, a career in the environmental industry can be your ticket to transforming the world!

You will need to be a keen problem-solver with a knack for science, and have a curious, questioning mind with a passion for all things green and sustainable.

Whether you want to work on a computer, or get out there and make progress in person, every working day in these eco-friendly jobs will bring you one step closer to creating a greener, cleaner, and brighter future.

Be an in-vitro meat producer

GROW ARTIFICIAL MEAT FROM ANIMAL CELLS

Picture yourself as part of a team of visionaries, equipped with state-of-the-art technology and endless creativity. As an in-vitro meat producer, you'll have the power to create artificial cuts of meat that taste just like beef, lamb or pork, but don't come from cows, sheep or pigs. This could mean a world where people can eat meat without harming animals or causing so much damage to the environment.

RECIPE FOR INNOVATION

Every day in this job, you'll get to blend scientific exploration with your culinary flair, pushing the boundaries of biology as you convert animal cells into tasty cuts of meat in a laboratory setting. You will also need to understand how to influence public opinion and be willing to explore ways to make lab-grown meat have everyday appeal to the average family.

FOOD FOR THOUGHT

Such a big change to our eating habits means people may question whether artificial meat is as tasty as the real thing, or whether it is safe to eat. With your scientific knowledge, passion for the environment and strong persuasive skills, you'll be ready to dispel people's doubts and show off the incredible benefits of this futuristic type of food!

TRULY BON APPÉTIT!

By pursuing a career in in-vitro meat production, you will help reduce or even stop the need to raise cattle, which is one of the leading causes of greenhouse gas emissions, conserve land and water resources (that would otherwise be used to keep farm animals), and promote animal welfare. Your work would have a real impact on creating a sustainable – and delicious! – future.

CRUELTY FREE·SAFE·HEALTHY ENVIRONMENTALLY FRIENDLY

LAB-GROWN MEAT

Be a coral reef gardener

DEEP DIVE TO PROTECT THE PLANET

Coral reefs are unique ecosystems bursting with colour and teeming with life beneath the waves. They might cover less than one per cent of the ocean floor, but they support over 25 per cent of all marine species. Sadly, overfishing, pollution, and climate change all pose serious threats to our coral reefs worldwide – which is why we need coral reef gardeners.

UNDERWATER WONDERS

A coral reef gardener is part biologist and part conservationist and they play a vital role in protecting these precious environments. By strategically planting small coral fragments and helping them grow and mature, the coral reef gardener actively contributes to helping damaged reefs return to full health. And, in turn, each thriving coral colony provides essential habitats for a huge variety of marine life – from tiny tropical fish to majestic sea turtles.

TEST THE WATER

Climate change means the ocean temperature is rising, causing coral bleaching (when corals turn white as they become less healthy). This means it's more important than ever to monitor reef health. You, the coral gardener of the future, will collect valuable data to support global research projects and conservation efforts. To excel in this role, you will have a passion for the ocean, know all about the science of corals and reefs, and how to care for these delicate organisms. And, of course, you will need to be a competent scuba diver, as your work will involve regular underwater expeditions.

BEACHY KEEN

Coral reefs exist in breathtakingly beautiful locations across the globe – from the Great Barrier Reef in Australia to the Coral Triangle in Southeast Asia – so it's a brilliant opportunity to do rewarding work while in a tropical paradise!

Meet real-life
CORAL PLANTER
Gabrielle Aisya

WHAT iS YOUR JOB?

Coral planting is kind of like gardening, but with a twist – I work underwater in the sea. Instead of planting flowers or vegetables on land, I help underwater coral reefs grow and thrive!

HOW DiD YOU GET INTO iT?

As a child, I loved the ocean and everything in it. As I grew up, I decided to study marine science at university, and corals captured my heart. I discovered that coral reefs aren't plants – they are actually animals!

I became a certified diver so that I could explore the ocean myself. It was during my diving adventures that I met my mentor, who offered me a job to help restore coral reefs.

"Coral planting is kind of like gardening, but with a twist – I work underwater in the sea."

TELL US MORE ABOUT YOUR JOB

Our main base for reef restoration is in Bali and Nusa Penida, Indonesia, where we have the most reefs planted. We also have other projects across the whole of Indonesia. Corals of opportunity are where we see corals broken to pieces by boats, by people standing on them, or by irresponsible divers – and we find diverse techniques to heal them by reading coral research journals, field checks, and trial and error. The methods we use to restore the reefs include building artificial reefs and drilling holes in stones then planting corals inside the holes, and much, much more!

HOW OFTEN DO YOU DIVE?

I dive often, sometimes to teach, sometimes to plant, sometimes to maintain and monitor the reef. The most diving I do is probably a full-month stretch twice every year for our coral instructor course. For this, I dive Monday to Friday for four weeks, learning everything from coral biology to reef restoration.

The preparation to dive becomes a routine. At first it was tough, diving from early morning to evening. But it is all worth it!

As well as being a confident diver and underwater swimmer, having a good understanding of marine science is another huge advantage. It helps you to figure out why some coral species are more challenging to grow, how different water conditions affect them, and what kind of environment is best for their growth.

WHAT ARE THE HIGHLIGHTS OF YOUR JOB?

Watching corals grow is like witnessing a tiny idea turn into something big and beautiful. When I come up with a creative way to help them, and when I see them developing from tiny pieces into vast colonies, it's incredibly rewarding.

Gabrielle planting corals underwater

HARNESS THE POWER OF WIND TO MAKE ENERGY

Wind power is an important part of the global shift towards clean, renewable energy. It means we can, over time, reduce our reliance on power stations with their harmful carbon emissions. By working in wind energy, you'll be a clean-air champion – combating climate change one gust at a time!

HIGH MAINTENANCE

You've probably seen wind turbines dominating the skies in the countryside or out at sea in floating wind farms, harnessing the power of the wind to generate electricity. As a wind turbine technician, you'll be in charge of these towering giants: climbing them to inspect the equipment, carrying out routine maintenance, and performing mechanical repairs as needed. While a background in mechanical or electrical engineering is useful, many employers offer on-the-job training.

GO LIKE THE WIND

The future is breezily bright for wind turbine technicians. With the world's growing need to switch to renewable energy, job prospects are soaring. It is predicted that by 2030, wind energy will be creating triple the current number of jobs in the UK and millions of jobs across the globe.

WHAT A VIEW

As for perks of the job, imagine waking up each day and heading off to a different landscape, with the great outdoors as your office. If you love staying active and have a head for heights, this is a job that will not leave you stuck behind a desk!

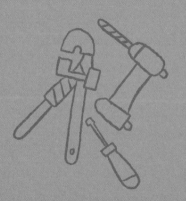

Be a forest scientist

STUDY THE WORLD'S GREEN SPACES

Forest scientists are securing the healthy future of our wooded areas, protecting biodiversity (the variety of animal and plant life in the world) and finding natural ways to fight climate change. Their research is used by governments and other decision-makers to manage our natural resources responsibly. That means not cutting down too many trees and ensuring new ones are planted.

Your day-to-day job would be studying forests and unravelling the relationships between plants, trees, animals, and their surroundings. You will be someone who loves nature and the outdoors, and enjoy combining different scientific areas, such as ecology, biology, and environmental science.

THE TECHNOLOGY OF TREES

Forest scientists use various tools and advanced technologies to conduct their research – like LiDAR, a light detection sensor that creates detailed 3D maps of forests. They might take tree samples to analyse the rings in a tree trunk and figure out climate patterns of the past, and they will use statistical models to make sense of the data they collect.

INTO THE WOODS

Much of your scientific life will take place in the tranquillity of nature. One day you might be exploring trails festooned with moss; the next, you could be heading off into unexplored forests to carry out ground-breaking research. Some of your time will also be spent computer modelling in an office or a lab. But wherever you're working, you'll be connecting with nature while contributing to global conservation efforts.

DID YOU KNOW?

Forests cover over 30 per cent of the Earth's land surface and provide a home for a staggering 80 per cent of all terrestrial species on our planet. Trees also do the important job of keeping our air clean of carbon. We need them now more than ever!

Be a bioplastic engineer

SOLVE OUR PLASTIC PROBLEM

The world has become hooked on plastic because it is cheap, convenient, can be moulded to almost any shape, and put to almost any use. But the problem with plastic is that it can take centuries to deteriorate, first breaking down into smaller pieces called 'microplastics' that pollute oceans and harm wildlife. Our need for sustainable alternatives has never been greater – and it's the job of bioplastic engineers to invent them.

BACK TO NATURE

Bioplastics are made from natural materials like corn starch, potato, seaweed or wood. They are already used to make packaging, like shopping bags and bottles, but can also be turned into clothes and even shoes. They can be manufactured with much less dependence on fossil fuels (oil, gas, and coal) and they degrade much faster than normal plastic.

MICROPLASTICS, BIG PROBLEM

Plastics are created by chemical reactions that can't be undone, which is why they take so long to break down. Bioplastic engineers have to understand materials to the molecule level. This is so they can figure out ways to make their inventions truly biodegradable – meaning they will decay naturally, quickly, and in a way that doesn't harm the environment.

THE SHAPE OF THINGS TO COME

Did you know, only nine per cent of all plastics are currently properly recycled? The ultimate challenge in getting our plastic problem under control is dealing with all the plastic that is already here! Scientists are developing some amazing solutions – using plastic-eating enzymes, converting plastic into fuel, and even turning it into building materials.

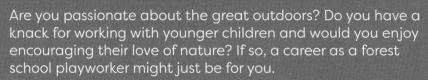

Be a forest school playworker

WHERE NATURE IS THE CLASSROOM

Are you passionate about the great outdoors? Do you have a knack for working with younger children and would you enjoy encouraging their love of nature? If so, a career as a forest school playworker might just be for you.

Forest schools are all about hands-on exploration, child-led play, and appreciating the joys of nature. As a playworker, your role is to create fun outdoor learning experiences for children of all ages in and out of school, while keeping them safe and happy. Insect scavenger hunts, forest walks, leaf printing, building fairy houses, cooking over a campfire, and woodworking are just a few of the things you might do!

COME RAIN OR SHINE

As a playworker, you'll be spending all of your days outside – whatever the weather! You will get to invent and present new games and adventures, using your imagination and creativity to come up with ideas that will spark the interest of the children in your care.

KEEP ON PLAYING

You will need to be a fountain of knowledge about all things nature-related, and will be keen to show young people how to enjoy, respect and nurture the natural world. Best of all, you'll get to keep playing every day – even when you're all grown up!

Be a green advisor

HELP PEOPLE CUT THEIR CARBON FOOTPRINT

Green advisors give expert advice and guidance on environmental issues, energy efficiency, and ways to live and work more sustainably. They work closely with families, households, and businesses or organisations to understand how they function. The advisor then produces a report giving tailored recommendations on how they could reduce their carbon footprint and lessen their negative impact on the environment.

To excel as a green advisor, you will need a solid understanding of environmental science and sustainability. You will stay up to date with the latest green technologies and the most recent developments in renewable energy.

GREEN THUMBS UP

In your role, you will assess how energy is used or wasted, identify areas for improvement, and create customised plans. You'll give advice on energy-efficient appliances, insulation, renewable energy, how to reduce the amount of waste you throw away, and how to use water more efficiently or sparingly. You will provide realistic and practical suggestions depending on your client's circumstances and help them see the benefits of adopting new habits that are good for the environment and will save them money.

A LITTLE GOES A LONG WAY

Making our world more environmentally minded needs to happen at every level – each of us can do our bit to save the planet. By working with individuals and businesses, where even a small adjustment may have a huge impact, green advisors are bringing about positive and important changes.

Be a bamboo farmer

GROW THIS SUPER SUSTAINABLE CROP

Bamboo is a type of grass that grows very fast, is remarkably strong, and has an amazing number of uses. It can be used in construction, furniture, and clothing and packaging. It's even being used to make more sustainable toilet paper! But most importantly, it's a renewable resource that is attracting attention worldwide – and we need people to grow it.

GROWING PLACES

As a bamboo farmer, your job is to manage bamboo plantations and nurture the potential of this remarkable plant. You will become an expert in the best growing conditions needed, including the right soil and climate, to ensure your plants are cultivated properly. Most bamboo plantations are located in tropical zones – although some species are now adapting to sunnier European climates around the Mediterranean Sea, so this is a field of interest that might take you places! It can be up to five years before a new plantation starts to produce ready-to-use bamboo, but you can gain experience and knowledge by working on established bamboo farms.

NO BAMBOOZLING HERE

Bamboo naturally doesn't need any pesticides or fertilisers to grow, and it uses less water than many other plants. This makes it a great alternative to those crops that require more time, effort and resources. So not only will you get the chance to see entire forests thriving under your care, but you will also know that your super-crop contributes to a greener and more sustainable world.

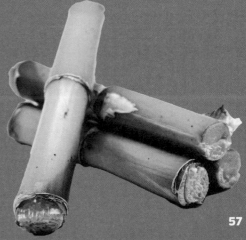

Be a satellite operator

GATHER KNOWLEDGE FROM SPACE

They may be out of this world, but satellites play a huge role in our daily lives here on Earth. These devices are sent up into space to collect and communicate information – connecting people worldwide through mobile and internet networks, guiding us to our destinations using GPS (global positioning systems), and helping us to forecast the weather. A lesser-known fact is that they are also able to tell us about the health of our planet.

EYE IN THE SKY

A keen interest in all things space, science and computing will serve you well as a satellite operator. You'll be in charge of collecting valuable data to improve our understanding of the Earth's climate and how it is changing. You'll be monitoring the state of the world's forests and their inhabitants, the effects of volcanoes, the extent of floodwaters, the spread of industrialisation, as well as the health of our oceans.

GREAT TRACK RECORD

In the early 1980s, satellites played a key role in identifying a thinning in the ozone layer over the South Pole. It led scientists to realise that it was harmful chemicals in everyday products that caused this problem. As a result, virtually all countries worldwide agreed to stop using them. Since then, satellite operators have continued to check on this 'ozone hole' and have seen encouraging signs that the atmosphere is slowly recovering.

GROUND CONTROL

The satellites might be in space, but the operators stay firmly on the ground! Working from advanced technology control centres, they can control and manage the systems, adjust trajectory and orbit, and fix any technical issues. In this job, not even the sky's the limit!

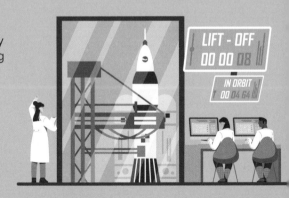

LIFT - OFF
00 00 08

IN ORBIT
00 04 64

Be a beaver ranger

PROTECT NATURE'S DAM BUILDERS

Reclaiming land for nature means allowing it to return to its original wild state. It's an important way to combat climate change. This includes reintroducing species long extinct, like the pine marten, bison, and even the clever beaver. In the UK, for example, beavers disappeared from the landscape hundreds of years ago because of hunting, but they are now ready for their comeback – with the help of beaver rangers!

SINK YOUR TEETH IN

The role of a beaver ranger is to protect the habitat of these toothy architects so they can live their life in the wild and do what they do best. Beavers are expert dam builders and bring many benefits to the environment: the ponds beavers create can slow the flow of rivers, filter the water, reduce the risk of flooding and drought, and encourage plants and other wildlife.

BEAVERING AWAY

A love of spending time outdoors and caring for wild animals is a must! A ranger will spend most of their day observing and protecting habitats by helping the beavers maintain

their dams when they are damaged by humans or violent storms. You will have little direct contact with the beavers themselves – they are crepuscular animals, which means they are only active very early or very late in the day.

LOOK OUT

Rangers also get to observe all of the other species of bird, fish and insect that thrive alongside beavers. You might also take visitors on tours in nature reserves, or you may visit schools to educate young eager beavers on the importance of protecting the natural world.

IF YOU'RE A *music* MACHINE...

When music resonates with an audience, it has the power to inspire, uplift, and connect people from all walks of life. If you want to pursue a musical career, there are chartloads of jobs out there – and they don't all require a music degree or perfect pitch.

Working in the music industry means being part of a vibrant scene, collaborating with musicians, producers and engineers, and coming across every other industry out there – where there is life, there is sound!

Some careers might require technical know-how or an understanding of music theory, while others are purely creative. You might help other people to make their music heard, or you could be creating the music itself. Some jobs can be done from the comfort of your own home; others will take you travelling all across the world. The possibilities are endless, and still developing every day.

SELL THE RIGHTS TO MUSIC IN FILM AND ON TV

Music is everywhere: in adverts, films, TV shows, shops, and on social media. We simply can't imagine a world without it, and it's only fair that creators and composers are recognised and paid for their work. Licensing agents are instrumental in making sure artists get the recognition and financial reward they deserve. They work closely with music publishers, record labels and advertising agencies, helping them to find the right music for movies, TV, video games and lots more.

NAME THAT TUNE

Licensing agents need to have a good understanding of the music and media industries, so that they can suggest music that will work best for particular projects – the perfect tune for a toothpaste advert will be different from the music for a tense and dramatic TV scene, for example. They have to be super organised to keep track of contracts, licences, and royalties (money paid to a composer or songwriter when their music is used by someone else). Not least, a licensing agent needs to be a 'people person' who can be the point of contact for artists and agencies.

COPYRIGHT THIS

Most importantly of all, licensing agents need to stay up to date with copyright laws and regulations, which protect musicians' rights and stop the illegal use of their music.

MUSIC TO YOUR EARS?

One of the most exciting parts of the job is discovering new talent and working closely with the artists and composers you represent. You will spend your days seeing live brands and listening to lots of tracks to find the music you feel truly passionate about.

Be a music therapist

USE THE HEALING POWER OF MUSIC

Listening to music can bring up all kinds of feelings, so it makes sense to use its power to help people through difficult times in their lives – which is exactly what music therapists do. They work with adults and children, using all kinds of musical styles and instruments to improve emotional wellbeing, reduce stress, boost confidence, build communication skills, and even ease physical pain.

STRIKE THE RIGHT CHORD

Finding the right words – or using words at all – can be very challenging for some people, either emotionally or physically. As a music therapist, you will need the ability to listen carefully to your patients, using your sensitivity to connect with their emotions and needs. Day to day, you'll run one-to-one or group therapy sessions, and you will check how your patient is progressing and if they're meeting their goals.

TUNE IN

Music therapists work in lots of different places: schools, hospitals, care homes and in private practices. They need to have training in music, psychology, and specific therapy techniques, but you don't need to be able to play ALL instruments to become a music therapist. Much of the job is about playing with sound and using music as a tool to communicate – this could be singing along, playing a simple melody on an instrument, or just moving to a beat.

DID YOU KNOW?

Music therapy has been around for a very long time. Ancient civilisations, like the Egyptians and Greeks, recognised and used the healing power of music.

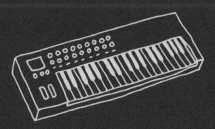

Meet real-life
MUSIC THERAPIST
Dr Ming Hung Hsu

WHY DID YOU CHOOSE TO DO YOUR JOB?

My love for music and my desire to help others have been the driving forces behind my journey as a music therapist and researcher. The idea of using music as a therapeutic tool to improve people's wellbeing really inspired me, and the potential to positively impact lives through the power of music drew me in.

HOW DID YOU GET INTO IT?

I completed my music therapy training at Anglia Ruskin University and achieved a Master of Arts degree. This qualification allowed me to practise as a music therapist in the UK, and my background in music – particularly my training as a classical baritone singer during my university studies – provided a strong foundation for this career. I use my skills and knowledge to help people with dementia in care homes manage their symptoms, and I work with staff on identifying triggers that worsen these symptoms, and how to ease them through music.

WHAT IS A SURPRISING FACT ABOUT YOUR JOB?

It's remarkable how many inventive and artistic methods can be put to use in music therapy. The power of music to form a bond with people is extraordinary, and discovering how different musical activities can positively influence people's emotions and behaviour is fascinating – not to mention very rewarding for me!

AND WHAT ARE THE BEST BITS ABOUT YOUR JOB?

Witnessing the power of music therapy on people's lives, particularly those with dementia, has been one of the highlights of my journey. Music can evoke memories, emotions, and connections that are often challenging to achieve through other means. It's incredibly fulfilling to know that my work improves the quality of life for these people and their caregivers.

"Music can evoke memories, emotions, and connections that are often challenging to achieve through other means."

CREATE REALISTIC SOUNDS FOR THE SCREEN

You're watching a film. You hear slow footsteps, thunder rolling overhead, someone breathing heavily... Nothing has happened yet, but you're already on the edge of your seat!

You might not pay much attention to a soundtrack when you're watching TV, but it's crucial for creating the right atmosphere. Choosing the right sounds and images while filming is close to mission impossible, and this is where the foley artist comes in. They create everyday sounds for the screen (film, TV and video games) and make them so realistic that the audience won't even think about them. This could be anything from a door slamming to a plane taking off.

YOUR IMAGINATION IN ACTION

The most fascinating thing about making these sounds is that very strange materials or objects are often used to achieve them! Coconut shells tapped together become horse hooves and the sound of paper being crumpled makes for a very convincing crackling fire. Creativity and attention to detail are needed to make things sound just right.

KEEP AN EAR OUT

As a foley artist, you will have a natural ear for sounds of all kinds and a serious imaginative streak. You'll be constantly on the look-out (or ear-out!) for real-world sounds and how they might work on screen. Understanding how acoustics work and how different textures interact is key – but getting the right sound is only half the skill! You need to be able to match it to what's happening on screen, to make sure the sounds and the visuals work together.

Be an audio engineer

GET TECHNICAL ABOUT MUSIC

Another often unsung hero of the audio world, the audio engineer, is the master of all things technical. They are responsible for editing and producing high-quality sound in a variety of settings, from working with musicians in recording studios, to managing the set-up and sound at live events.

A lot of the job is about working with acoustics. Think about how your voice sounds in a tiny room compared to outside in the open. It simply doesn't sound the same. Audio engineers are at the heart of making live music or human voices sound 'right' no matter the venue. They will take into account how sound reacts to the particular size and shape of space, then use their mixing skills to balance and adjust the sound quality.

TOP OF THE TECH

Audio engineering is all about the right consoles, software, and sound gear. Schools and community centres often have studio set-ups that can help you get a feel for the kind of tech you might love, and you can always test out your ears at home! You could practise with samples of your own music, and experiment with editing the sound by using a phone, tablet or a computer, even adding cool sound effects.

MIX IT UP

Audio engineering as a skill is rising in demand. If you love how music sounds in different settings, this could be a booming opportunity for you. As well as working within the music industry, there are also opportunities to work on films, TV shows, audiobooks, or podcasts – so it's worth keeping your ear to the ground about this brilliant career.

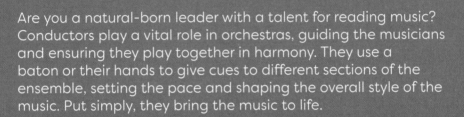

Be a conductor

GUIDE ORCHESTRAS TO PLAY IN HARMONY

Are you a natural-born leader with a talent for reading music? Conductors play a vital role in orchestras, guiding the musicians and ensuring they play together in harmony. They use a baton or their hands to give cues to different sections of the ensemble, setting the pace and shaping the overall style of the music. Put simply, they bring the music to life.

WHAT'S THE SCORE?

To become a conductor, you will need to have a solid understanding of music theory and be able to read sheet music at a glance. You'll also need excellent communication skills to express your interpretation of the music to the orchestra. A keen sense of rhythm and a good ear for pitch are also key to maintaining the musical flow.

PIECE BY PIECE

Most professional conductors start their careers by conducting smaller ensembles or amateur orchestras and gradually progress to larger orchestras, opera companies or musical theatre productions. But the job goes beyond performing. You will plan musical programmes and decide which pieces to perform. A large part of the job will also involve running rehearsals and training musicians ahead of shows.

TAKE THE STAGE

Much like musicians, conductors have their own personal styles – but these are expressed through hand gestures, body language and facial expressions rather than instruments. That means the same music can sound quite different from one conductor to the next! Some are known for their energetic movements, while others have a more restrained and precise approach. Although they don't face the audience, make no mistake: conducting is performing.

Be a tour manager

GO ON A ROUND-THE-WORLD ROAD TRIP

A tour manager is the brain, eyes and ears behind epic music tours, creating unforgettable experiences for both the artists and the fans. If you have a passion for music, a knack for organisation, and a thirst for adventure – this could be the job for you.

MUSICAL MASTERMIND

As tour manager, it's your job to make sure the schedule runs smoothly – everything from arranging travel plans and coordinating with concert venues, to managing money and organising interviews. You will handle all the behind-the-scenes magic, so the musicians can concentrate on their bit – making music!

HIT THE ROAD

Touring involves lots of travel, which can be physically and mentally exhausting. Your crew will be grateful for proper pit stops and a chance to see something other than the inside of a tour bus! And it's not just about organisation, but resilience too. Delays and cancellations do happen, so you'll need to stay calm under pressure and flex those problem-solving skills to make sure the tour keeps rocking.

ALL-ACCESS PASS

It can be a demanding job, but it's also full of rewards. You become part of a big, musical family that inspires and supports each other – sharing the highs and the lows while going on a globetrotting adventure together, doing what you love!

Be a luthier

CRAFT GUITARS AND OTHER STRINGED INSTRUMENTS

Have you ever wondered how guitars are made, or who makes them? A luthier is someone who builds and repairs stringed instruments like guitars, violins, and ukuleles. They typically work in workshops, alone or as part of a small team. It's the pitch-perfect job for combining a love of music and craftsmanship – concentrating on single instruments, not mass production.

PULL THE STRINGS

If you love making things, have an eye for detail and a good ear for music, you could train as a luthier. You will learn how to shape and carve wood, select the right materials, and assemble all the different parts of an instrument. Patience and precision are crucial as you will work on fiddly tasks like fitting the strings, adjusting the bridge (the piece of wood that supports the strings), repairing dents or fractures, and fine-tuning the instrument to create the perfect sound.

MAKE IT SING

Wood, brass and strings are materials that all react differently to sound, and it takes real skill and musical talent to understand their physical properties and make an instrument sing beautifully. Did you know that each guitar has its own unique voice? Luthiers experiment with various woods to achieve different tones and characteristics. Some guitars are made from exotic woods, like rosewood or mahogany, while others use more common woods, like spruce or maple.

LABOUR OF LOVE

Luthiers may spend weeks or even months creating a single guitar or violin, adding intricate details and decorations. Each handcrafted instrument will be totally unique – a true work of art that will then go on to help musicians create their own artistry.

Be a ghost songwriter

WRITE SONGS FOR OTHER ARTISTS

What if you have lots of stories you want to put into song, but no desire to perform them on stage? What if you want to transform your thoughts and experiences into lyrics, but don't want to sing them? What if you could hear your favourite artists playing your songs, and get paid for it?

Ghost songwriters are the hidden talents behind the music, writing songs on behalf of other artists or record labels. They can either work as a team with fellow songwriters, or on their own.

HIT THE RIGHT NOTE

To become a ghost songwriter, you'll need to be able to understand and capture the essence of an artist, carefully crafting lyrics and melodies that align with their unique voice and musical style. It's also important to network and meet people in the industry to get your songs in front of the right people.

CHANGE YOUR TUNE

The beauty of being a ghost songwriter lies in the freedom it offers. You can work across different genres and collaborate with a diverse range of artists. Though you won't get all the credit, there's satisfaction to be found in exploring lots of musical avenues and hearing your words resonate with people all around the world.

SPINNING TALES

And the best part? You don't need heaps of qualifications. What you do need, though, is a deep passion for music, a mastery of language, and a knack for storytelling. So sharpen your writing skills, immerse yourself in different genres, and let the music move you.

Be a sonic brander

CREATE SOUND SIGNATURES FOR BRANDS

Sounds are embedded in our everyday life to the point where we might not even notice them – but pay attention to the beeps, jangles and short melodies around you. Think about the feelings they bring up. Do they sound urgent or calming, scary or reassuring? Because sonic branders think very carefully about the effect these sounds have on you.

SONIC SIGNATURE

Sonic branders are masters of sound who create distinctive audio identities for big companies. They figure out how the company wants to come across, then turn this into short but unforgettable melodies, known as sound logos or jingles. These are played in TV or radio ads to catch the attention of audiences and make their brand instantly recognisable. Just like how seeing a logo makes you think about a company, so does hearing particular sounds... It's sound DNA!

SOUND-SCAPING

By skilfully arranging music, choosing instruments, and using advanced audio techniques, you can craft sound environments that create brand experiences, bring back memories, and evoke emotions.

LISTEN UP

Sonic branding is an art that combines creativity, psychology, and technical expertise – and you will want to hone your listening skills. Pay attention to the sound logos of brands you like, record them and ask people how the sounds make them feel – you'll learn loads and get experience under your belt!

Be a sign language interpreter

TRANSLATE SONGS INTO SIGN LANGUAGE

Music has the power to unite us, but it doesn't always speak to everyone in the same way. Deaf and hearing-impaired individuals might not get to experience melodies and lyrics – but this is where music sign language interpreters come in. These professionals translate the beauty of music into visual gestures and signs, making it accessible to all.

MUSIC IN MOTIONS

Music sign language interpreters serve as bridges between the hearing and non-hearing communities. Their work allows Deaf and hard-of-hearing individuals to enjoy live concerts, music festivals, and music videos, broadening the audience for musicians and fostering inclusivity across the industry.

GIVE ME A SIGN

To succeed in this role, the first step is to master sign language! There are lots of different sign languages across the world, so you'll need to know the right one where you want to work. You'll also need an in-depth knowledge of music genres and an appreciation for the emotional nuances of each. Interpreting music is an art in itself, and you must think creatively to capture the essence of a song through signs.

HELPING HANDS

This job comes with challenges, like interpreting complex lyrics and translating emotional intensity, but the rewards are profound. Enabling Deaf individuals to experience the magic of music is a meaningful and creative pursuit that enriches the lives of interpreters and those they serve.

IF YOU'RE GREAT WITH GADGETS...

In the fast-paced and interconnected world we live in, technology has become an indispensable part of our daily lives. It has revolutionised industries, enhanced communication, and transformed the way we navigate the world.

Jobs in tech have emerged as some of the most sought-after and promising career options in recent times, and their importance is expected to grow even further in the future.

To excel in tech jobs, you'll need a combination of problem-solving skills, analytical thinking, and creativity. You will need to become a whizz in programming languages and data tools, and never be afraid of adapting to new technologies as they continue to move at lightning speed.

Be a cryptographer

KEEP PEOPLE SAFE ONLINE

In today's technology-driven world, cryptographers are making the internet a safer place. Their job is to develop encryption software, which is a type of security program that protects the data you send and receive online. It keeps all that information private – everything from personal details, like credit card information, to business transactions, such as confidential emails.

GET WITH THE PROGRAM

Cryptography will appeal to you if you're mathematically minded, talented with tech, and have a knack for creative problem-solving. On the job, you will need to stay up to date with the latest programming languages (sets of commands that deliver instructions to your computer) and strong analytical skills will help you identify potential weaknesses in code so you can develop stronger encryption methods.

SAFETY IN NUMBERS

Cryptographers work across a number of industries, including the government, finance, tech, and research. Day-to-day tasks may include developing new methods for encrypting data, deciphering encrypted messages, and testing security systems against potential cyber threats. Pursuing a degree in computer science will be useful, but self-taught programmers can also find themselves excelling in this career – practice makes programmers!

DID YOU KNOW?

Coding has a rich history, dating back to ancient civilisations. Julius Caesar, for example, used a simple code called the Caesar Cipher to encrypt military messages. This is a substitution method where letters in the alphabet are shifted by a certain number of spaces – a shift of 1 would mean A becomes B, B becomes C, C becomes D, and so on.

Be a robotics engineer

MAKE INTELLIGENT MACHINES

When it comes to tech jobs, robotics engineers are at the forefront of innovation. They specialise in the design, development, and maintenance of robotic systems. Essentially, they bring machines to life, creating smart robots that are revolutionising industries and improving our daily lives. If you dream of engineering the future and unleashing the potential of AI, then robotics might be the right career path for you.

ROBOTS TO THE RESCUE

Robotics engineers work across a wide range of industries, where they design robots to perform tasks that are repetitive, difficult, or dangerous for humans. They might develop robotic arms for manufacturing, self-driving trucks for transportation, or humanoid robots (meaning they look like humans) for medical research. Robotics engineers are also behind the self-flying drones used for aerial photography and even search-and-rescue missions.

FICTION TO FACT

Robotics has roots in science fiction, inspiring past and present generations with visions of intelligent machines. Many blockbuster films are full of classic examples of robot engineering, droids with various tools, and abilities well beyond human capacity! These ideas from fiction are taking shape in reality thanks to robotics engineering here, today, in our own galaxy – not too far away after all!

CYBORG SKILLS

Becoming a robotics engineer requires a strong foundation in science, technology, and maths. A degree in mechanical engineering, electrical engineering, or computer science can provide an excellent starting point – and building up top-notch coding skills will be crucial for programming productive robots.

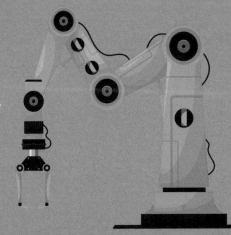

Be an app developer

CREATE APPS FOR PHONES AND COMPUTERS

Did you know, about seven billion people worldwide own a mobile phone? So it's no surprise that demand for app developers is on the rise. These are the people who design and build the mobile applications used on phones and computers. If you're tech-savvy, have an eye for design, and fancy creating the next TikTok, this could be the app-solute perfect fit.

TECH TASKS

As an app developer, you might find yourself developing new apps from scratch, and writing code to test how well they work across various devices (for example, on phones versus larger screens, like tablets and desktop computers). You will test your software to find and fix potential faults and update and improve your apps on a continuous basis in response to customer feedback.

USER EXPERIENCE

One of the most important factors in app development is user experience (UX for short), which is how pleasing an app is to use. Being able to create visually appealing apps that offer a seamless, trouble-free experience for the customer is the name of the game – so, as well as coding skills and knowledge of computer science, creative thinking is key.

STAGGERING NUMBERS

Back in 2008, there were only about 500 apps available on the app store; today, there are millions! And the demand for apps will just keep on growing...

Be an ethical hacker

OUTSMART CYBER CRIMINALS

'Malicious hacking' is when people break into computers without permission, with the intention of stealing private information and causing harm. It's against the law. 'Ethical hacking' is the opposite. It's when hacking is used to identify vulnerabilities in systems so they can be fixed – turning the hacker's skills into a force for good!

SUPER HACKERS

Ethical hackers are hired by businesses that handle sensitive data – especially banks and government institutions – to find and fix weaknesses in their computer systems, networks, and applications. They do this by carrying out 'penetration testing', which is an authorised hack on software that mimics a real-world attack, helping hackers and their clients spot gaps in security.

Ethical hackers also help companies by taking part in bug bounty programs. This is when companies put a call out for testers to find flaws and weaknesses in specific software or websites, and hackers put them to the test and get paid cash rewards for what they find.

DIGITAL DEFENCES

You might be engaged by a financial institution to perform a security assessment of their online banking platform, identifying potential weak points and advising on ways to reinforce their defences. You might also collaborate with a government agency to test their security against cyber threats.

HEROES AND VILLAINS

Did you know, malicious hackers are also known as 'black hat hackers' while ethical hackers are called 'white hat hackers'? This is a reference to old Western films, where the good guys wore white hats, while the bad guys wore black!

Be a nanotechnologist

USE TECHNOLOGY TO WORK ON TINY INVISIBLE PARTICLES

Nanotechnology, the science of the incredibly small, is changing the way we live, work, and play. Nanotechnologists use their expertise to manipulate matter at the tiniest scales imaginable – the nanometre level, where one nanometre is about 100,000 times smaller than the width of a human hair.

MIGHTY MINI

One of the many remarkable things nanotechnologists do is create super-strong materials like graphene, which is stronger than steel and incredibly thin. Imagine a bike helmet that's not only lightweight but also incredibly tough, thanks to these nanoscale reinforcements. In the electronics world, nanotechnologists create smaller and more powerful computer chips. This means faster and more energy-efficient devices, like smartphones and laptops that fit in your pocket.

LASER FOCUS

Nanotechnologists also work their magic in medicine. They develop nanoparticles that can deliver drugs precisely to cancer cells, to reduce side effects and increase the effectiveness of treatments. These tiny particles can even help detect diseases earlier through ultra-sensitive diagnostic tests.

MASS BENEFITS

Environmental heroes, nanotechnologists develop filters that clean water and air by removing pollutants on a nanoscale level. They are also working on solar cells that are more efficient, potentially powering our homes with clean energy.

Becoming a nanotechnologist requires at least a bachelor's degree in a science or engineering field, like physics, chemistry, materials science, or electrical engineering. You'll also need to be a master problem-solver and enjoy working in high-tech labs with specialised equipment. Precision is also a must when working at such small scales!

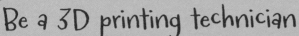
Be a 3D printing technician

TURN DIGITAL DESIGNS INTO PHYSICAL OBJECTS

Are you passionate about technology and love making things? Why not consider a career as a 3D printing technician? These are the experts who operate and maintain 3D printers, a type of cutting-edge technology that lets you turn digital designs on a screen into physical objects in the real world.

HARD COPIES

Working as one of these technicians, you would start by creating a 3D digital model of the object you want to make. The 3D printer then 'reads' this design and starts printing liquified plastic layer by layer, building the object from the bottom up. This is left to cool and solidify, before you can clean, sand, and polish your object.

SUSTAINABLY BUILT

In the past, models could only be made by removing or cutting down material from a larger piece, creating inevitable waste. Modern 3D printing is known as an 'additive process' – this means it builds up an object, layer by layer. This is a much more environmentally friendly approach, as it uses every bit of material.

3D OPPORTUNITIES

3D printing is used for incredible things. In medicine, it might be used to make custom replacements for people who have lost a limb. Astronauts in the International Space Station use 3D printing to create tools and parts without having to rely on getting them sent from Earth, making their space missions easier and safer.

DID YOU KNOW?

3D printing is not limited to plastic. Lots of other materials can be printed too, like stainless steel components for aerospace, or concrete for constructing buildings. Ceramics can be 3D-printed to make lace-like pottery, or chocolate can be turned into delicate sculptures.

Be a virtual reality engineer

CREATE iMMERSiVE EXPERiENCES

Imagine putting on a headset and being instantly transported to a fantastical world where every detail feels so real you can almost touch it. That's exactly what virtual reality (VR) can do; it's a type of computer technology that uses images and sounds to make you feel like you're somewhere else. It's the job of VR engineers to create these hyper-realistic experiences – designing, developing, and testing new technologies that blur the lines between the digital and the physical.

A NEW (ViRTUAL) REALiTY

VR is often associated with video games and other forms of entertainment, but it is also changing the way we take care of our mental and physical health. For example, if someone is really scared of heights or speaking in front of a crowd, therapists can use VR to create pretend situations where they can face those fears. This helps people get over their fears in a safe and controlled way. The future of VR will also revolutionise tourism, taking us to far-flung destinations and remote wonders of the world – all without leaving the comfort of our living rooms.

IMMERSE YOURSELF

Every day, VR engineers use their skills in coding, 3D modelling, and working with other technicians to design and improve virtual worlds. If you have a passion for gaming, virtual reality experiences, and computer graphics – plus curiosity about pushing the boundaries of technology – you might be a great fit for a career in VR engineering. But you'll need to get a degree in computer science first!

Be a video game tester

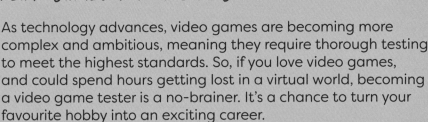

PLAY GAMES FOR A LIVING

As technology advances, video games are becoming more complex and ambitious, meaning they require thorough testing to meet the highest standards. So, if you love video games, and could spend hours getting lost in a virtual world, becoming a video game tester is a no-brainer. It's a chance to turn your favourite hobby into an exciting career.

Video game companies hire skilled testers to identify bugs, glitches, and story issues before releasing their games to the public. They write up reports making recommendations for improvements, providing valuable feedback that helps to make games better for all players worldwide.

TESTING, TESTING

A passion for gaming is more important here than formal qualifications. Begin by thoroughly playing and testing the games you already play. Pay attention to details, such as graphics, gameplay, and bugs. Document any issues you encounter. Many game developers offer beta testing phases for their games before the official release. Sign up for beta tests of games that interest you and provide feedback on your experiences.

STAY FOCUSED

But it's not all fun and games! Being a video game tester is a dream for many, so there is a lot of competition. It requires plenty of patience, plus attention to detail for spotting bugs and issues, and good communication skills for documenting exactly what those issues are. Testers often work to tight deadlines, so playing at a leisurely pace may not be an option!

PLAY PERKS

As well as getting to play games before their official launch, testers get a behind-the-scenes sneak peek at the creative process – getting to see how a game evolves from an early, rough version to the final, polished release.

Meet real-life SENIOR GAME DESIGNER Magali Stretton

WHAT DO YOU DO iN YOUR JOB?

I am a game designer for Crystal Dynamics, the company who develops the Tomb Raider games. Prior to that, I worked nine years at Rocksteady Studios on the Batman Arkham games. When I was younger, I loved the Tomb Raider games so it's crazy to think that I am now working for the company who made these games! Developing games is like making a movie or writing a book. It's a creative process. You start with an idea, and then you have constraints to work within, like time and budget.

My job is to create the levels of a game, meaning I take the story lines set by the game and narrative directors and I turn them into playable experiences, working with teams of animators, artists, coders and more. The hardest part is to get all the details just right, and so you need testers to be constantly testing your game. In my experience, a good tester is worth their weight in gold. Not only do they find problems, but they can help you solve them too. Testers are essential to making a great game!

HOW DiD YOU GET STARTED?

At school, I was quite good at maths, but my passion was film, so that's what I went to study at university. But I missed mixing creativity and maths, patterns and logic. I felt like a failure when I realised film wasn't for me. But you can really grow as a person when you learn from what didn't work. One day, I got an opportunity to learn about how video games were made. I was always a gamer, but it hadn't even occurred to me that this could be a job! I met people that showed me that video gaming was a serious business – not just something 'techy people' do on the side. It blew my mind. I felt that this was my calling. I decided to study game design for a year while working. Once I got a portfolio together and my CV updated, I sent them to recruitment agencies. It was the foot in the door I needed, and amazingly, Rocksteady Studios offered me a job as a junior game designer.

WHAT iS A HiGHLiGHT OF YOUR JOB?

We worked very hard for two and a half years on Batman Arkham City, following the success of the first one (Batman Arkham Asylum). There was a lot of pressure to be just as good – and we did it in the nick of time. On release day, we got top reviews. I felt such a deep sense of joy, sharing that moment with my co-workers where you feel like you've made something people really love.

iF YOU WANT TO WORK iN ViDEO GAMES...

If you're a gamer you might think you can't work in gaming because you don't know how to code, or you might not be good at maths. But this is a multi-billion-dollar industry and there are so many different jobs that there might be one for you! From writers, illustrators, animators, 3D artists, concept artists, voice-over artists, stunt actors, community and social media managers – and if you are good at maths, there are plenty more jobs for you too. If gaming is your passion, you can make a career out of it. Just work hard, keep focus and most importantly... follow your heart!

A game designer at work on the design of a video game

"Developing games is like making a movie or writing a book. It's a creative process."

Be an astrobiologist

STUDY LiFE BEYOND EARTH

Astrobiologists are the pioneers of an extraordinary field. Their mission? To investigate the possibility of life on celestial bodies beyond Earth. If we ever plan to establish human colonies on the Moon, Mars, or even further into space, we need to understand how the conditions there might support our species. That makes astrobiologists the key players in our quest for extraterrestrial living.

OUT OF THiS WORLD

In their search for life across the universe, astrobiologists spend most of their time in laboratories on their home planet! They will test and record different kinds of bacteria to see how they survive in extreme conditions, as well as looking at fossils of the earliest life forms to investigate how they may have arrived on Earth. Some astrobiologists will even search for signs of intelligent life in space through radio signals or satellite images. Yes, that means aliens!

SHOOT FOR THE MOON

To succeed in this career, you'll need a solid foundation in biology, astronomy, and environmental science. Technical know-how and problem-solving skills are a must, as you'll be thinking up innovative solutions to unexpected obstacles. A sense of wonder and an unquenchable thirst for exploration are qualities that set astrobiologists apart.

GIVE SPACE A CHANCE

Astrobiologists typically work with research institutions, space agencies, and universities. Successes in the field include growing plants aboard the International Space Station and exploring conditions in extraterrestrial environment simulations on Earth. Just think, these exciting breakthroughs may one day lead to a whole new way of life!

Be a genetic genealogist

USE DNA To TRACE FAMiLY HiSToRiES

Genetic testing looks at our genes, which carry the information that determines which characteristics are passed on to you by your parents. They essentially act like your body's instruction manual! This kind of testing helps doctors and scientists find out if we have certain genes that can make us sick or affect how we respond to medicines. It can also tell us about our family history and our ancestors.

FAMiLY TREES

Genetic genealogists unveil the hidden stories within our DNA, enriching our understanding of where we come from. Their job is to combine DNA testing and genealogical research to trace family lines and paint detailed pictures of a person's heritage. Day to day, these experts analyse DNA test results, sift through historical records, and piece together intricate family trees. They may reunite separated families, uncover long-lost relatives, and even assist in cold cases by identifying unknown suspects through genetic markers!

SCiENTiFiC SLEUThiNG

As well as an in-depth understanding of genetics and biology, you'll need excellent research skills, attention to detail, and patience as the work often involves meticulous detective work. Compassion and sensitivity are also crucial when helping people uncover potentially life-changing information about their origins.

DiD YOU KNOW?

Genetic testing is a fairly new area, thanks to major breakthroughs in DNA research. In 2003, scientists completed the Human Genome Project, which mapped the sequence of about 25,000 genes that make up a human being's DNA – making the science accessible to all, helping us to better understand and prevent diseases, all while improving our knowledge of genetic diversity.

IF YOU WERE
BORN TO PERFORM...

Are you a natural performer who enjoys nothing more than getting the rapt attention of an audience? Are you yearning for a career that uses your acting, singing, or dancing talents (or all three)?

Being passionate about performing opens doors to lots of exciting professions where you can channel your creativity and charisma into your work. This could involve public speaking, creating and performing your own shows, entertaining a street audience or carrying out daring stunts – the possibilities are endless.

To succeed in these unconventional careers, you will need lots of confidence, be able to think on your feet and have a genuine love for connecting with others through performance.

TAKE YOUR MOVES TO THE STREETS

Street dance is a constantly evolving art form, mixing amazing acrobatics with lots of different social dance styles – from hip-hop, popping and locking, to breaking, waacking and krumping! If you've mastered those moves, or fancy giving them a try, street dancing could be the job for you.

Emerging from the urban communities of the United States over the last 40 years, what started as a personal passion has since blossomed into a recognised career across the entertainment industry. Nowadays you can be paid to perform in music videos, movies, TV shows and live concerts, or even be part of a renowned dance crew.

STRENGTH AND STYLE

Street dance demands impressive physical strength, flexibility, and creativity. While some professional dancers have formal dance training, many dancers are self-taught, honing their skills through years of practice. They might use online videos to learn new styles and participate in competitions like dance-offs or jams as they develop confidence.

BREAK FREE

Success as a professional street dancer lies not only in learning the dance techniques, but also in building your own signature style and storytelling through moves.

Individuality and freshness are key! You'll study and create your own choreography, as well as working in a group with other dancers, musicians, and artists.

MAKE YOUR MARK

You'll need the confidence to do some self-promotion, whether that's recording and sending out footage of your routines or preparing for and attending auditions in person. Many dancers and crews have their own performer names and logos, which can really help to set you apart from the crowd.

Be a barrister

PERFORM IN A COURT OF LAW

A barrister is a lawyer who specialises in representing clients in court. This might not seem like performing at first – but think about the courtroom as a stage and things start clicking into place! A successful barrister needs to present their case convincingly. This requires serious debating skills, as well as the ability to capture and keep the attention of an audience. Like actors, lawyers must immerse themselves in their roles, understanding the nuances of their case so they can deliver compelling arguments to sway the judge and jury.

ACTING OUT THE LAW

Did you know, legal firms often recruit individuals who have studied drama? These candidates bring valuable courtroom-ready skills, easily adapting to the high-pressure atmosphere of many trials. Being able to improvise allows a lawyer to think on their feet, exude confidence and navigate tense situations – all crucial skills in the world of law.

MOCK TRIALS

During their legal training, law students often take part in mock trials. These pretend trials allow students to practise their advocacy skills (this means the ability to speak supportively on another person's behalf) and present cases in a formal courtroom setting.

MEMORISE THIS

Actors need to learn lengthy scripts by heart before performing them flawlessly in front of an audience. The same is true for lawyers! They need excellent memories to remember all the complicated details of their cases and present them accurately.

Be a historic re-enactor

PERFORM iN THE PAST

What if you could step out of the present and immerse yourself in scenes from history? Historic re-enactors are time travellers of sorts. They are actors who adopt the personas of famous figures from days gone by, dressing in historically accurate costumes and transporting us to different times. Imagine stepping into the shoes of a Civil War veteran rallying troops, a medieval knight engaging in a chivalrous duel, or a suffragette passionately advocating for women's rights. These performers bring history to life, giving us a front-row seat to the past.

HiSTORY REPEATS iTSELF

By giving life to historical characters and events, re-enactors make history accessible and relatable for modern audiences. They might work in living history museums, heritage sites, or educational institutions. They may also participate in local and national historical events or work as historical consultants for film and television productions.

ACT THROUGH THE AGES

Great historic re-enactors are most often history enthusiasts with a flair for performance and an eye for detail. Research is the key to authenticity, so you will need to know your character inside out to express yourself in the language and mannerisms of the time. You'll need to be comfortable improvising and keep your wits about you as you answer questions from the public.

GROUP PERFORMANCE

Re-enactors need to adapt to different conditions as well, from vast outdoor venues to indoor museum exhibitions. Collaboration and a strong sense of community are often at the heart of their work, as re-enactors share their passion for history and support each other in creating engaging historical retellings.

Be a master of ceremonies

HOST GLAMOROUS EVENTS AROUND THE WORLD

Large events – like awards ceremonies, business conferences, and charity fundraisers – can be challenging when you have dozens or even hundreds of people attending. As the master of ceremonies (usually known as 'the MC'), you're in the spotlight on stage from beginning to end – opening the event, warming up the audience, introducing speakers, delivering important announcements, and keeping the energy high. A big part of your job is making sure the event stays on schedule, so everything happens in the right order and at the right time.

LOUD AND PROUD

If you want to be an MC, being a confident public speaker is a must! You will also need to be organised, as you'll need to prepare for events ahead of time – meeting with organisers to learn about the overall event and the line-up, then writing engaging, well-structured scripts that will maintain the flow.

QUICK WIT

Live events can be unpredictable. As an MC, you must be quick on your feet and able to handle unexpected situations with ease.

In case of any technical glitches, for example, you will need to stay calm. A sense of humour goes a long way – with jokes and stories at the ready, you'll be able to connect with your audience and lighten the mood when things don't go to plan.

GOING PLACES

Being an MC means lots of variety in your work. One day you might be hosting a fancy wedding reception in a formal garden; the next you could be presenting an industry conference in a five-star hotel. Plus, events can take place anywhere in the world – so be prepared to travel near and far.

READ SCRIPTS TO ENTERTAIN AND INFORM

Have you ever been told that you have a voice that could charm birds out of trees? Well, maybe you should put those soothing tones to the test and look at becoming a voice actor. In this job, you'll create the narration for all types of media – from audiobooks to animated films. That means you could become the reassuring voice in a nature documentary, the persuasive voice-over in an advert, a quirky character in a cartoon, or even a sinister villain in a video game!

SOUND WORK

A typical day on the job might involve auditioning for a new project, attending a recording session in a soundproofed studio, or brainstorming with directors and producers on the best way to bring scripts to life. These specialist actors also often find themselves lending their voices to unexpected projects – like speaking the directions for a GPS system or recording the public announcements for amusement parks!

HONE YOUR VOICE

The ability to interpret scripts, convey emotions, mimic accents, and adapt to different styles and situations is essential. Voice actors must be versatile and possess impeccable diction, breathing control, and microphone techniques – all skills that can be honed in drama school. You can also spend time listening to your favourite 'voices' and learn from them in your own time!

NOW YOU'RE TALKING

As for perks of the job, there are plenty. If you love performing but get camera shy, it can feel like a less pressured form of acting – as you do it entirely offstage and offscreen. Plus, unlike theatre or film actors, you can read directly from the script and don't need to learn your lines by heart, so an excellent memory is not in the job description!

Be a stunt double

STEP IN FOR ACTORS DURING DANGEROUS SCENES

Lights, camera, action! When you watch an epic car chase or a complicated fight scene on film, you're likely witnessing the work of talented and extremely brave stunt doubles. They are trained professionals who step in for actors to perform the dangerous sequences that leave audiences on the edge of their seats.

THE ROAD LESS TRAVELLED

The path to becoming a stunt double is rarely conventional. Many of these daredevil doubles have a background in athletics, martial arts, gymnastics, or some other physically demanding discipline – with a thirst for adventure leading them to the world of stunt work.

BALANCING ACT

This is as physical a job as it gets, so keeping fit, strong and nimble should be high on your list of priorities! To execute jaw-dropping stunts, you'll need excellent coordination, precise timing, and the ability to learn complex choreography. Whether you're performing stunts high up in the air or deep underwater, each and every one should be thrilling, authentic and (despite what the audience sees) completely safe!

SEEING DOUBLE

Even though your face won't be seen on screen (thanks to the use of clever camera angles and editing techniques) you'll still be performing. When stunt doubling for a particular actor, you must match your movements, mannerisms, and expressions to those of the character you are impersonating, to create the illusion that you are the same person.

Be a cruise ship entertainer

A VOYAGE OF DISCOVERY AND DRAMA

Are you dreaming of a career that combines passion for performance with thirst for travel? Look no further than becoming a cruise ship entertainer. This glamorous lifestyle offers a unique opportunity to showcase your all-singing, all-dancing talents while travelling the world. But what is it really like on board?

KNOW THE ROPES

Cruises offer a working environment like no other: the sea sets the scene, and the ship is your stage. Whether you're a dancer, singer, magician, musician, or comedian, you'll need to be a confident and experienced performer (with good sea legs!) who knows how to captivate an audience. It can help if you speak other languages too, as passengers and crew members will come from all over the world.

BOAT SWEET BOAT

Cruises vary in length – some might only last a week, but others will last several months, so be ready to make the ship your home away from home for whole seasons at a time. It can be demanding work, as you'll be expected to work long hours entertaining passengers, but you'll still have plenty of opportunities to soak up the ship's leisure facilities.

SET SAIL

This profession is truly an adventurer's dream. Wake up to beautiful sunrises in far-flung destinations and explore new cultures during day trips on land. As one of the ship's passengers (even if you are a working one!), you'll get the same amazing benefits – witnessing the wonders of the world, from ancient ruins to modern metropolises, all while living out your dream job.

Be an aerialist

PERFORM ACROBATICS IN THE AIR

Have you ever dreamed of defying gravity? Of soaring through the air with grace and agility? Being an aerialist is exactly that – using physical strength, fearlessness, and flair to perform incredible acrobatic routines high above the ground. Although they have been mainly associated with traditional circuses in the past, aerialists have found their place in the modern world of entertainment, adding a touch of enchantment to music festivals, theatre performances, and even corporate events. They often work for troupes or get hired for specific shows.

FLYING HIGH

First and foremost, mastering the art of aerial performance demands exceptional physical skill – flexibility, strength and coordination are essential as performers must navigate trapezes, hoops, and ropes in the air with fluidity and precision.

MAKE THE LEAP

Dedication and concentration are also needed. Aerialists must undergo rigorous training to learn proper techniques and be able to follow strict safety procedures. Most aerialists will start by training as gymnasts, dancers or going to circus school.

ACTOR IN THE AIR

For aerialists, performance is at the centre of the craft – they must look elegant and effortless while performing physically demanding feats. It's a breathtaking combination of artistry and athleticism that leaves audiences in awe.

Meet real-life AERIALIST Jackie Le

WHAT IS YOUR JOB?

I'm a circus artist. My main skill is as an aerialist, performing on different apparatuses like silks, hoops, rope, loops and hair hanging.

HOW DID YOU BECOME AN AERIALIST?

I used to work long hours as an office manager during the day, in an unhappy work environment. I started trying out different hobbies like going to the gym, rock climbing, martial arts and then stumbled upon circus classes for adults at the National Centre for Circus Arts (NCCA) in London and fell in love. I spent all my free time attending lessons in mainly ground-based skills like handstands, acrobalance and tumbling. One day I saw someone do a drop on silks and I wanted to do that too.

Although I didn't have a background in dance or gymnastics, after six months of learning rope and silks, I was accepted for professional training at NCCA and a year later was invited to perform on a stage in front of an audience for the first time. From that moment, I have never looked back. Shortly after, I quit my office job. It wasn't easy at first, but I have finally and successfully made being a circus artist my full-time job.

"It was magical to be surrounded by such wonderful artists, performing in a cool show in a traditional circus tent."

WHAT DO YOU LIKE ABOUT YOUR JOB?

I love that my job gives me the freedom to choose my own hours and keep things interesting, whether it be performing in a local London venue or flying across the globe hanging from spectacular arenas. Being at home during the day and teaching/performing in the evenings works for my family's lifestyle.

My work is varied: I have been on tour and had shows running for a while in one venue, working with female acrobatic troupe Mimbre in their show 'The Exploded Circus'. Performances also range from children's shows to cabaret for older audiences.

I've been performing for nearly 15 years and I still train really hard to keep at a standard to wow audiences. Sometimes it is exhausting, but I try to not let that show on or off stage.

WHAT ARE YOUR FAVOURITE THINGS ABOUT YOUR CAREER?

I've had many wonderful jobs, and sometimes it's not just about the performance but the atmosphere. Last year I was in a Halloween show called 'Hag' and they took such good care of us. It was magical to be surrounded by such wonderful artists, performing in a cool show in a traditional circus tent. I cherish the lifelong friendships I have gained from travelling across the world.

Jackie performing with silks

Be a stand-up comedian

MAKE PEOPLE LAUGH FOR A LIVING

The lights dim, the spotlight shines, you land your first punchline, and the laughter begins – that's the life of a stand-up comedian. But it's not just about telling jokes; it's an art form that combines great writing, reading people, and working a crowd. Stand-up comedy is a solo performance, meaning it's just you and your microphone on the stage, so it's not for the faint of heart – but those with a cracking sense of humour and a talent for entertaining will find it incredibly rewarding.

FUNNY BUSINESS

Successful comedians are fantastic writers who always look on the funny side of life, with an uncanny ability to spot those odd, everyday moments that can be turned into comedy gold. Beyond the writing, performance is the heart and soul of this profession – confidence, comedic timing, and stage presence are vital to delivering side-splitting anecdotes and witty one-liners.

JOKING AROUND

Great stand-up routines require lots of practice, but it's also important to be able to think on your feet. Understanding the audience's mood and adapting your set accordingly can turn a simple set of jokes into an extraordinary experience. Open mic nights (live events where anyone is allowed to take to the stage and tell some jokes) are a great way to practise these skills before you book your own gigs.

ON THE ROAD AGAIN

Expect to spend a large chunk of your working life travelling to different venues and staying in hotels as you take your show on the road. It might sound fun (and it is!) but it can get tiring, so you'll need to take lots of breaks to keep your comedic mind fresh.

Be a pyrotechnician

CREATE SAFE AND SPARKLING FIREWORK DISPLAYS

If you always 'ooh' and 'aah' at fireworks displays, you might fancy a career as a pyrotechnician. They are the technical magicians behind breathtaking firework displays at concerts and other celebratory events, lighting up the night sky and dazzling their audiences.

SAFETY FIRST

To succeed in this job, you will need to blend creativity with technical understanding of fire and explosives. Making sure your show is safe for the performers, the crew, and the audience is the most important part of the job. You will need to know about the various chemicals you are using and work within strict safety guidelines and local laws. Fireworks are dangerous, so caution and attention to detail are key.

PLANNING A FIRE SHOW

Pyrotechnicians collaborate with event organisers and designers to understand their show requirements, create themed displays, and synchronise fireworks with music. This requires organisation and coordination, using specialist computer programmes to deliver a seamless and shimmering display according to very precise timings. They are also responsible for setting up and dismantling the displays.

YOUR TIME TO SHINE

Now for the fun bit! When the moment to perform arrives, a pyrotechnician takes their turn in the spotlight. With nerves of steel, they run the show – hitting each cue flawlessly and transforming a carefully orchestrated plan into a stunning spectacle. The true skill of a pyrotechnician lies not just in their ability to manipulate light and colour, but in their capacity to create unforgettable moments for all to cherish.

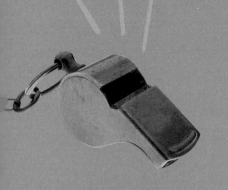

IF YOU'RE A SPORTS FAN...

Pursuing a career in sport is the dream for many people, but it's important to remember that there are many more opportunities in this energetic field than just being a top player.

Whether it's coaching, scouting, journalism, sports psychology, or even sports medicine – there are plenty of possibilities to be found off the pitch, with each role playing an integral part in shaping the sporting world.

So, if you live and breathe sport – but are not necessarily hungry for a spot on the winner's podium – these careers will allow you to inspire others, help athletes and teams succeed, raise awareness of your chosen sport, and make a lasting difference.

KEEP THE GAME FAIR AND SQUARE

Referees are guardians of the official rules of their sport, overseeing games and ensuring that all players and teams abide by them. By upholding fairness, impartiality and, if necessary, penalising foul play, referees promote good sportsmanship, discipline, and healthy competition.

PLAY BY THE RULES

Being a professional referee is not for the faint of heart. It's a job that requires strong character, an in-depth understanding of the game, and the ability to make split-second decisions. If you're ready to step onto the field, court or pitch and start calling the shots, grab your whistle and let the games begin!

BEYOND THE WHISTLE

Referees prepare for games by getting to know the participating teams and athletes, and inspecting the playing field. During the match, they must be vigilant, watching for fouls or violations.

Referees have to be expert communicators to explain their decisions, keep players calm, and maintain control of the game. Post-match, they may also provide feedback and constructive criticism to help players and coaches improve.

KEEP UP

As well as being mentally sharp, referees need to stay physically fit to keep up with the players! Even between games, they're always on the move. They travel from stadium to stadium, for local leagues and international tournaments, overseeing different games and adapting to the specific demands of each one.

Be a video assistant referee

USE TECH TO SUPPORT FAIR PLAY

Speaking of playing by the rules, referees have a new high-tech ally: the video assistant referee (VAR for short). VARs are operators who use cutting-edge video replay technology to help referees make accurate decisions during all sorts of games: football, rugby, boxing, cricket, and tennis. They closely analyse critical moments – from allowing penalties that can make or break a team's chances, to ruling on a foul line in a dramatic match point, they are often involved in nail-biting and emotionally charged situations.

ALL ANGLES

VARs work in teams of three or more in a control room within the stadium. This is equipped with multiple screens displaying different camera angles and replays. They review and compare footage to provide real-time feedback to the referee on the playing field.

THE DECIDER

This is a fast-paced and demanding role where you get to combine your love of sports with advanced technology. It requires quick thinking, an eye for detail, and the ability to operate the tech at lightning speed. Much like the referee, you'll need a solid understanding of the sport's rules and regulations, and you must be able to remain calm and confident under pressure – as your decisions may be questioned by coaches, players and fans, and could potentially influence the outcome of a game!

FASTBALL

VAR tech does have some limitations; it can only rule on specific aspects of a game – but it's the most exciting ones! In football, that includes goals, penalties, red cards, and mistaken identity (for example, if the referee sends off the wrong player). In table tennis, where the ball can travel at 110 km per hour, VAR technology is not fast enough to keep up!

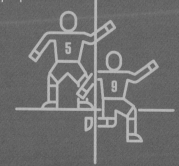

Be a personal trainer

HELP PEOPLE GET FIT AND HEALTHY

If you love being active and enjoy helping others, becoming a personal trainer might be the perfect path for you. This job involves creating workout routines for clients – but it's not just about muscle-building; it's about inspiring good habits and supporting people to lead a healthy life, in body and mind.

IN TRAINING

Imagine you are a personal trainer, and you have a new client. You will start by assessing their fitness levels, their strengths, and areas for improvement by taking them through simple but challenging physical tests. Based on this information, you will design a tailored fitness plan that suits their needs, demonstrating proper exercise techniques so they can work out safely and effectively. You may also provide a nutrition plan – many personal trainers are trained nutritionists, too – to help your clients understand how to balance their meals to support their physical efforts. Whatever services you offer, your aim is to create a supportive atmosphere where people feel encouraged and motivated to achieve their goals.

FLEX YOUR TIME

Some trainers work in gyms, wellness centres or even outdoors in public parks, while others offer virtual training sessions. You will probably see your clients regularly, once or several times a week, working around their availability. But flexibility is one of the perks of the job – it's not a nine-to-five career, so you can decide when you are 'open for business'.

STRENGTHEN THE STARS

Athletes and fitness-conscious celebrities often have dedicated personal trainers to help them stay in shape. As an A-list actor's personal trainer, for example, you could be tasked with helping them get ready for a physically demanding role – like playing an ultra-fit superhero in a movie!

Be a sports journalist

WRITE ABOUT YOUR FAVOURITE SPORTS

Sports journalism is an exciting career choice for those who are always watching, reading about, or talking about sports. These specialist journalists write up sporting events for the media and often have front-row seats to truly historic moments – like World Cup wins and Olympic records. Their job is to capture the energy of these electrifying events, then share it with the world in their own words.

BREAKING NEWS

The perks of being a sports journalist include access to exciting behind-the-scenes events (like press conferences with famous athletes), travelling all around the world and, most importantly, getting paid to watch your favourite sports live in action! You could find yourself interviewing your childhood hero or flying overseas with your favourite team, reporting on what it takes to play sport at the very highest level. The best way to get started is to get stuck in, write your own stories, make your own videos on social media, or offer to cover events for your school or local team!

BE PART OF THE STORY

Sports journalism is so much more than reporting on scores and stats. You'll need to be a great storyteller, able to write captivating accounts that inspire and thrill fans. You'll need excellent investigative skills, too, diving into athletes' lives to uncover their struggles, their triumphs, and their journey to the big leagues.

A SOCIAL SPORT

The future of sports journalism is bright. Digital media has opened up new opportunities through podcasts, live streaming, and social media. Successful journalists often engage directly with fans online, building a loyal following and establishing themselves as respected, knowledgeable voices in the industry.

Be a golf ball diver

FIND AND FETCH LOST GOLF BALLS

Within the realm of sporty professions, one intriguing and lesser-known occupation is that of a golf ball diver. Golfers often hit stray shots that land in ponds, lakes, and other bodies of water, so professional golf ball divers are hired to plunge into these watery depths and retrieve them. This career combines two hobbies – scuba diving and golf – to improve the sustainability of the sport, keeping our waters clear and giving golf balls a longer life.

A NEW BALL GAME

You'll need to be a trained scuba diver with superb swimming abilities, physical fitness, and excellent eyesight for searching in murky waters. The job demands stamina and perseverance, as divers often have to contend with challenging conditions, like low visibility and freezing temperatures, to recover a lot of golf balls. Each body of water on a golf course can contain thousands of lost balls! In the USA alone, an estimated 300 million balls end up underwater every year!

GREENER GOLF

Golf ball divers are like professional, underwater recyclers! The recovered golf balls are typically cleaned, refurbished, and resold, providing an affordable and eco-friendly alternative to purchasing them brand new. Their service benefits both golfers and golf course owners, maintaining the cleanliness, playability, and sustainability of the course, while also providing a steady source of income for professional divers.

Be a talent scout

DISCOVER AND NURTURE BUDDING ATHLETES

As a talent scout, you'll have the amazing opportunity to shape the future of sports. Your job is to recruit talented new athletes to professional clubs – which means you get to be the person to spot the sporting world's next star player. Their work contributes to the growth and success of sports teams and provides amazing opportunities for aspiring athletes to make it big.

A STAR IS BORN

A day in the life of a talent scout typically involves attending games, tournaments, or training sessions in schools and colleges to check out aspiring athletes. They look for individuals who possess the magic combination of natural talent, physical prowess and mental toughness that is needed to play sport at the highest level. They collaborate with coaches, agents, and team managers, providing them with comprehensive scouting reports and recommendations.

SPOTTING GREATNESS

Talent scouts specialise in specific sports, so you'll need unparalleled knowledge of your sport of choice. Talent scouts often start by playing or coaching sports, then move on to scouting as they gain experience and connections in the industry. Excellent attention to detail will help you assess an athlete's physical skills – including strength, speed, agility – and their overall athleticism. Plus, communication and negotiation skills are essential for successfully getting the right athletes into the right club.

GLOBE TROTTER

Talent scouts often travel around the world in search of promising athletes. A European football club scout found a talented young player from a remote part of South America. Impressed by the player's exceptional skills, the scout arranged a trial and helped the player join a professional football club. That player? None other than Lionel Messi.

Be a Formula 1 tyre changer

TEAMWORK AT LIGHTNING SPEED

A Formula 1 team's pit crew operates like a well-oiled machine – without them, no driver would get to cross the finish line. The tyre changers are particularly important; although tyres are built for extreme speed and performance, they get worn out on the racetrack within minutes! The tyre changer's goal is to change the car's tyres quickly and flawlessly during a super-speedy pit stop. For this, you need to be agile and focused. You need to get some serious mechanical skills under your belt and show your knowledge of all things motorsports.

READY, SET, go

Before a race, you will prepare the tyres by heating them up and checking for any damage, choosing the best tyres for the track conditions. On the day, you'll use power tools and wrenches that can turn at incredible speeds to remove the old tyres and attach new ones. Pit crew teams are made up of about 20 people, with each tyre changer having a specific role, either working on the front or rear tyres – one tyre alone requires three changers working on it at the same time!

NOT JUST SPEEDY MECHANICS

Tyre changers need to have in-depth knowledge about tyre technology, compound (the rubber mixture making up tyres), and very precise measures, like how well specific tyres perform in terms of speed, traction, lasting power and how much fuel they burn. This expertise enables them to make informed decisions at speed during races, adjusting tyre pressures and optimising the car's set-up for different tracks.

EVERY SECOND COUNTS

Each Formula 1 race will have between one and four pit stops – and, astonishingly, they last no longer than two or three seconds!

Be a cycling tour guide

LEAD GROUPS OF TOURISTS ON YOUR BIKE

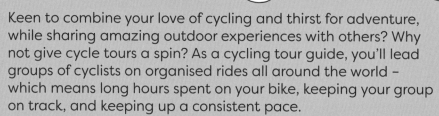

Keen to combine your love of cycling and thirst for adventure, while sharing amazing outdoor experiences with others? Why not give cycle tours a spin? As a cycling tour guide, you'll lead groups of cyclists on organised rides all around the world – which means long hours spent on your bike, keeping your group on track, and keeping up a consistent pace.

READY TO ROLL

You'll need physical fitness, endurance, and the ability to handle different terrains and weather conditions. Flexibility and adaptability are also crucial, as you may encounter unexpected challenges, like dealing with sudden weather changes, gears breaking down, traffic issues, or injuries that require quick thinking and problem-solving. Additionally, thorough knowledge of geography, local customs, and bicycle mechanics are all essential for providing a smooth and enriching experience for your fellow cyclists.

FREE WHEELING

Being a cycling tour guide provides a refreshing sense of freedom from everyday routine – it's as far away from a desk job as you can get! You'll explore new places, breathe the fresh air, and embrace the beauty of nature, all while sharing your passion for cycling with like-minded bikers.

RIDE OF A LIFETIME

Whether it's riding through the stunning French countryside, climbing the ancient ruins of Machu Picchu in Peru, or pedalling along the rugged coastlines of New Zealand – your cycling career will take you to some of the most awe-inspiring places on Earth, with each route presenting a fresh adventure.

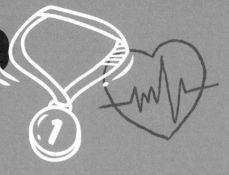

Be a sports scientist

HELP ATHLETES REACH THEIR FULL POTENTIAL

Science plays a crucial role in the world of top-level sport, unlocking human potential and pushing the boundaries of athletic achievement. As a sports scientist, you will study the scientific factors that influence health and exercise – working with athletes to improve their performance, prevent injury, and enhance overall wellbeing.

CHOOSE YOUR FIELD

In sports science, you can explore various ways to help athletes get better and stay healthy. Physiology looks at how the body works during exercise, biomechanics studies movement, nutrition examines diet, sports psychology deals with the mental side of sports, and performance analysis uses data to improve athletic performance.

GET ON THE PROGRAMME

To become a sports scientist, you will need a degree, as well as strong people skills and great attention to detail. Your focus will be on working with athletes to identify their strengths and weaknesses. You might provide guidance on the best times to eat specific nutrients, how to avoid or recover from dehydration, or what supplements to take to maximise energy levels. You may also consult with doctors to rehabilitate an injured athlete. Staying on top of any new research will also ensure you offer the best support.

STOP, WATCH

Sports scientists use clever tools like wearable sensors and performance-tracking software to collect and analyse data from training sessions, measuring progress and providing evidence-based reports to athletes and their coaches. This scientific approach has led to remarkable performance gains, from faster sprint times to increased endurance levels.

Be a skydiving instructor

GUIDE THRILL-SEEKERS THROUGH PLANE JUMPS

As jobs go, it doesn't get more thrilling than jumping out of planes every day! Skydiving instructors teach people the basics of skydiving, taking students thousands of metres up in the air and guiding them through their first jumps. Beyond that, professional instructors can work as coaches, helping repeat jumpers to improve their technique as they work up to more challenging dives.

FREE FALLING

A typical skydive lasts between five and seven minutes from exiting the plane to landing on the ground, with the free-fall portion usually lasting around 30 to 60 seconds. You'll experience a thrilling adrenaline rush and a sense of weightlessness, reaching speeds of up to 200 km per hour before pulling the parachute. Once the parachute is open, the descent becomes much slower, allowing you to enjoy a more relaxed ride while taking in the view.

SAFE LANDING

But it's not all about the jump! You'll also be packing the parachutes and ensuring all safety protocols are followed, especially in changing weather conditions. You will also need to be a great people person and a strong communicator, reassuring nervous jumpers and building confidence before they take the leap.

JUMP INTO ACTION

To be an instructor, you'll need lots of training to become an expert skydiver yourself first. Beginners have to start by making tandem jumps (meaning you are strapped to an instructor), and then progress to jumping solo. You will need to complete a set number of skydives to demonstrate your abilities and safety awareness, as well as take written exams to obtain your instructor's licence.

Meet real-life
PROFESSIONAL SKYDIVER
Ben Wood

HOW DID YOU GET INTO IT?

Since I was 18 months old, I followed my dad around the country while he was doing parachute displays. I would sit at the drop zone watching all these colourful parachutes in the sky and seeing how much fun everyone was having. Three days after my 16th birthday (you have to be 16 to skydive), I did a tandem skydive from 12,000 ft with my dad jumping out of the plane beside me and flying down to shake my hand in free fall at 120 mph. Surprise, surprise – that was me hooked on skydiving! I have been around skydivers my whole life and I've been actively jumping out of planes for over 30 years now.

WHAT EXPERIENCE DO YOU NEED?

Although I did well at school, you don't actually need any academic qualifications to jump out of a plane! All you need is someone to drive you to the airfield, and money to get a lift to 12,000 ft above the ground.

WHAT IS A SURPRISING FACT ABOUT YOUR JOB?

Anyone can do it! At the club on the weekends, you could be skydiving with a lawyer, a delivery driver, a police officer, and a world champion – and you might not even know it because everyone is just there to skydive.

It doesn't matter who you are or how much money you have, everyone is there for the same reason – and once you're qualified with a licence, you can go anywhere in the world and skydive.

WHAT ARE THE HIGHLIGHTS OF YOUR JOB?

I've won national championships and worked with TV celebrities. I was the first ever person to skydive in front of Mount Everest and also achieved the highest ever parachute landing on the same jump.

Family means a lot to me, and to share my hobby and career with them is fantastic. I was lucky enough to have my dad teach me how to skydive, and I've taught my son how to do it too – I'm not sure there are many third-generation skydivers out there!

Having my youngest son waiting for me when I'm performing a skydive display into a beach, or his grandad and I skydiving into his under 9s football match as they were warming up to wish him luck, are just two highlights I've experienced with my own sons. My youngest son is now working at the drop zone with me every weekend, just like I did as a boy. I'm also running my own skydiving business in Cornwall, with my brothers, partners, friends and little helpers – I love my job so much that it never feels like a 'chore'!

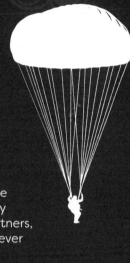

"I was the first ever person to skydive in front of Mount Everest!"

Ben during a free fall

115

IF YOU HAVE A *passion* FOR FASHION...

Behind the glitz and glamour of the catwalk, there are plenty of opportunities to pursue 'backstage' in the fashion world. When people say a 'career in fashion', you might immediately think of clothes designers and runway models – but there are many more roles out there to suit a range of skills, interests, and qualifications.

From bustling design studios and high-end boutiques to film-set trailers and fast-paced magazine offices – you could find yourself working in some fabulously fashionable workplaces.

Creative and energetic, these environments are often buzzing with passionate individuals who set trends, blaze trails, and live and breathe the latest styles.

CREATE TEMPLATES FOR FAB FASHION

If you have a passion for fashion and a keen eye for detail, pursuing a career as a pattern maker could be your perfect fit in the fashion industry. Pattern designers create the templates that show designers and manufacturers how to make products like clothing, shoes, and even furniture. These templates ensure that the products look consistent when made in large quantities and across different sizes (known as mass-production).

MADE TO MEASURE

A typical day as a pattern maker is a blend of communication, creativity, and precision work. You might meet with product designers and sample makers to discuss requirements. You'll create templates, measuring and cutting patterns in the right material – then double and triple check those measurements! You'll review final products and check in with designers to make sure you're turning their ideas into reality. It's the art of turning fabric into fashion, and every stitch counts.

SEW TECHNICAL

Pattern makers combine their artistic flair with technical expertise to get the job done. While patterns used to be drawn by hand, nowadays, pattern designers mostly use cutting-edge software – like CAD (Computer Aided Design) – to create drawings, modify templates, and store patterns digitally.

DID YOU KNOW?

Pattern making has a rich history. Before standardised sizing arrived, master pattern makers were highly sought after by rich individuals who could afford to have their clothes tailor-made.

Be a make-up artist

A CAREER IN COSMETICS

Does the thought of working with make-up for a living make you blush with excitement? Make-up artists transform people's appearances using cosmetics – whether that's enhancing a runway model's features with flawless make-up, or working with actors in film, TV or theatre. They are make-up magicians who can make dark under-eye circles 'disappear' and transform clean faces into creative characters with just a few strokes of a brush.

FACE TIME

As a make-up artist, you could end up working in lots of different places. Fashion weeks (international events where designers show off their latest collections) are a busy time for make-up artists, where steady hands are hired to glam up models swiftly and skilfully before they take to the catwalk. Behind the scenes in film or TV, make-up artists work with costume designers to bring all kinds of characters to life, ensuring their make-up will look great on camera and last through long days on set.

LIP SERVICE

In this job, you'll be getting up close and personal with models and actors to make them look their best, so communication skills are just as important as cosmetic ones. You'll want to create a calming and cheerful atmosphere through lots of chit-chat so that your clients (and their face muscles!) can relax.

GLOW UP

Did you know that make-up artists often work their magic to make actors appear sweaty on TV, when the bright studio lights aren't doing the job? For scenes involving action or exercise, their challenge is to create the perfect fake glow – thankfully without the smell!

Meet real-life
MAKE-UP ARTIST
Olivier Chauzy

HOW DID YOU GET STARTED?

Being a make-up artist wasn't really a job that existed when I was growing up. It was the 80s, fashion was all about big hair and big make-up and I used to do make-up for myself and my friends. When I left school, I trained as a hairdresser, but then I had a bad car accident that meant I couldn't be on my feet in a salon for months and I got very bored. My brother had friends in a band who were about to make a video for one of their songs, and they asked me to help create their looks. I found lots of samples and went on set with them. I loved it all. I was hooked and I wanted more. I managed to sign up for the very first training course in professional make-up in my town. It was three months long and extremely expensive, but it was worth it. Armed with my new diploma, I called any photographer or production company I could find and offered my services. It took some serious courage to pick up the phone to strangers over and over again and hear a lot of 'no's!

WHAT DO YOU LOVE BEST ABOUT YOUR JOB?

I love that it's the opposite of an office job. It's unconventional, you work strange hours and you never really know what your next job is going to be, but I find that exciting.

Make-up is a very personal artistic form of expression – working with other creative talents like directors and photographers to translate what they are trying to achieve, while bringing your own style. It's also a career in which you are constantly learning on the job – each project is a chance to try something different, work with someone new and learn from them.

WHY iS THiS THE RiGHT CAREER FOR YOU?

I'm a real social butterfly which is essential in this job as it means working one-on-one with different people all the time. Sometimes I work on my own, sometimes in a team with other make-up artists and hairdressers. On a recent film, I worked in a team of over 100, creating the look for a huge cast of historical characters with incredible costumes. It felt like I was literally walking through time.

You have to be good with people and also quite mindful and discrete. Sharing a skin-to-skin relationship with actors or models means they can feel very vulnerable, so it's important for make-up artists to create a sense of trust.

Top tip:
don't believe the hype! Influencers who share make-up tips often only know their own face. When you are a professional make-up artist, the trick is to be able to work with new faces all the time.

Olivier applying make-up during a shoot

Be a product stylist

MAKE ANYTHING LOOK GOOD

Whether it's online, on TV, in magazines or splashed across billboards, advertising is everywhere – and the work of a product stylist is always at the centre.

Their job is to make products like clothing and accessories look irresistible, carefully arranging them during photoshoots so that the images you see in catalogues and glossy magazines make you want to buy the products.

MUST-HAVES

Whether they work with fashion or food, home decor or tech gadgets – product stylists have an eye for design, colour, and the latest trends, allowing them to breathe life into inanimate objects. They work closely with art directors and photographers in studios, using different lighting, props, and backgrounds to transform ordinary spaces into extraordinary shots. They might set up a sleek, shiny metal surface to showcase the latest smartphone, or surround an eco-friendly shampoo with beautiful plants. They may also work on location, near or far from home, attending outdoor photoshoots – so the ability to make products look fabulous in all types of weather is a must!

SOCIAL BUTTERFLY

You will also need to be marketing-savvy to understand what will catch people's attention across different platforms – from print ads and press releases to websites and social posts. If social media feels like a second home to you, you're off to a stylish start!

TRICKS OF THE TRADE

Did you know, product stylists have a bunch of tricks up their sleeves to get picture-perfect results? They use hidden supports, pins, and tape to create illusions, so even the most ordinary of products, like a simple bottle of water, can be arranged in exciting and original ways, such as making it appear as if it's pouring into a glass in mid-air.

MAKE FASHION ECO-FRIENDLY

'Fast fashion' is the business of making cheap clothes quickly to take advantage of the latest trends. Low-cost, fashionable clothing might sound good, but it comes at a heavy price that is paid by the planet – creating a lot of waste when these clothes are quickly thrown away. This is why we need sustainability officers in the fashion industry. They are hired by fashion brands and manufacturing companies to help make clothing more sustainable and suggest ways to reduce their impact on the environment.

CAMPAIGN FOR CHANGE

You will spend time researching and sourcing more eco-friendly materials that are good for the planet, like organic cotton, linen or bamboo, which don't rely so heavily on pesticides or chemicals to be made. Then there will be the not-so-small matter of convincing manufacturers to change their process! You may also work with marketing teams on campaigns to encourage customers to recycle their clothes instead of throwing them away.

MAKE YOUR MARK

To become a sustainability officer, you should care about the environment, be good at solving problems, communicate well, enjoy working with others, and be happy juggling lots of data. You will want to gain a degree in environmental science or sustainability. You could then intern in fashion companies and work your way up the job ladder.

SUSTAINABLY SOURCED

Nowadays, high-street consumers want to know where their clothes come from, and they are more likely to look for sustainable options. Part of the job of sustainability officer is to help people make better decisions when buying clothes – raising awareness of the dangers of fast fashion, and promoting clothing that's made in an eco-friendly and ethical way.

TRACK TEXTILES THROUGH TIME

Did you know, not all libraries are full of books? A fabric librarian blends a love of textiles and history, creating and managing a 'library' of fabric samples from different cultures and time periods. These libraries are an important resource for budding designers as they learn about the history of the fashion industry and develop their own ideas, providing inspiration for the design of clothes, accessories, and even soft furnishings (like curtains or upholstered furniture).

FABRIC OF THE JOB

You'll want a degree in textile, fashion or library science, and will need to look for any opportunity to gain experience working in fabric collections. Daily tasks for a fabric librarian include classifying, cataloguing, and organising textile samples by date, colour or era. They often handle delicate fabrics and antique embroidery, so they need to take extra care and know the right techniques to preserve them. As a textile librarian you will conduct your own research as well as answer questions from the general public or industry professionals, or work alongside researchers looking for information. Your work might also take you to museums, fashion archives, or textile research institutions.

LIFE'S RICH TAPESTRY

Textile librarians also collaborate with fashion designers, historians, and curators to source textiles for museum exhibitions, showcasing the rich heritage and evolution of fashion. Through their knowledge and expertise, they can help to recreate historical garments and educate others on textile techniques from earlier times.

Be a wardrobe organiser

HELP PEOPLE CURATE THEIR CLOTHES

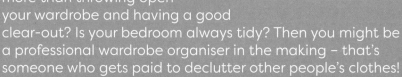

Are you the person your friends turn to when they need help rifling through clothes and deciding what to wear? Do you love nothing more than throwing open your wardrobe and having a good clear-out? Is your bedroom always tidy? Then you might be a professional wardrobe organiser in the making – that's someone who gets paid to declutter other people's clothes!

EVERYTHING IN ITS PLACE

Imagine curating the perfect wardrobe for your client, so they have all their clothes at their fingertips. Your organisational skills can be a lifesaver for busy professionals who don't have time to tidy their overflowing cupboards. You might be helping them declutter, categorise belongings, store seasonal clothes or start using clever solutions like shoe shelves or storage bins. A great organiser will know the art of being tactful and positive to make people feel happy in their newly organised home.

TIDY CLOTHES, TIDY LIFE

Wardrobe organisers create spaces that reflect their clients' lifestyle (and fashion style!), helping to declutter and optimise their wardrobe. Research has found that the average person can spend anything from a few minutes to several hours every day dealing with laundry and choosing their clothes. Imagine saving them just 10 minutes per day and over 10 years, you are giving them an impressive 25 days of their time back!

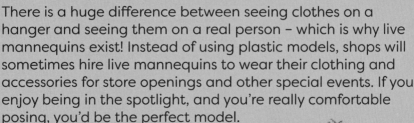

Be a live mannequin

STRIKE A POSE

There is a huge difference between seeing clothes on a hanger and seeing them on a real person – which is why live mannequins exist! Instead of using plastic models, shops will sometimes hire live mannequins to wear their clothing and accessories for store openings and other special events. If you enjoy being in the spotlight, and you're really comfortable posing, you'd be the perfect model.

MODEL BEHAVIOUR

Dressed in designer clothing, you'll strike captivating poses and show off the latest fits. Though we often think of models as working on runways, this job might take you to department stores, promotional events, and fashion exhibitions. More and more clothes companies are also producing videos of live mannequins wearing their products to use in advertising.

BOOK OF LOOKS

If you're interested in getting into live mannequin work, you'll need to start by building a modelling portfolio that showcases your talent for presenting clothing and accessories effectively. It will generally be an online collection of photos that you can share easily with agencies. A well-curated social media platform can become your calling card. Modelling agencies do not only focus on high fashion models, they also need people with the right look on their books that the general public can relate to.

Be a runway choreographer

DIRECT FASHION SHOWS

If you're looking for a career that lands somewhere between theatre and fashion, why not consider runway choreography? It's like being a director, but instead of plays or films, you're in charge of fashion shows! As a runway choreographer, it's your job to make sure the latest fashion is showcased in the most captivating way possible on the catwalk. You'll coordinate all the different elements of the show – everything from music, lighting, and set design, down to the way in which the models walk.

TOP MODELS

Fashion shows may look flawless, but they can be a bit hectic behind the scenes! Runway choreographers make sure everything runs seamlessly. In this role, you will work closely with fashion designers and stylists to bring their vision to life, and you'll train models to move with confidence and grace – choreographing sequences and specific poses to show off the designer clothing they're wearing in the best possible way. Attention to detail is crucial, as you'll need to synchronise the models' movements with the music and lighting.

FIRST STEPS

Building your career often starts with assisting established choreographers or interning with fashion event producers to learn the ropes. As you gain experience, build a portfolio of your work and network within the fashion industry to be first in line when opportunity knocks. Developing your unique choreography style and staying updated with fashion trends will help you stand out.

JET-SET LIFESTYLE

Your days will be filled with rehearsals, fittings, and meetings with the entire fashion team – working together to refine and perfect the show. You might find yourself jetting off to New York, Paris, Milan, and other fashion hotspots, working with world-renowned designers and experiencing the energy of international fashion shows.

Be a trend analyst

SPOT THE NEXT BIG STYLE

In the ever-changing world of fashion, getting ahead of the next big trend is essential for success. That's where trend analysts come in. Through market research and expert pop-culture knowledge, they help fashion brands predict what will sell next season. If you live and breathe fashion, this really is the job for you.

FASHION FORECAST

Trend analysts are the eyes and ears of the fashion industry, forecasting what will take the retail world by storm. Their days are spent researching and processing all kinds of data: consumer behaviour, cultural influences, important events, new technologies, and social media crazes across the world – all the things that could have a direct or indirect influence on fashion. It's the analyst's ability to take in all this information and identify common patterns that makes them so valuable to product designers, clothing companies, and other fashion aficionados. Formal education in fashion design or marketing will be a great stepping stone, as well as building your experience through internships with fashion companies or magazines.

ON THE LIST

A trend analyst might work for all kinds of organisations, like fashion brands, agencies or magazines, retail companies, or be a freelance consultant providing trend insights and forecasts to all of the above! Whichever path you find yourself following, you will be at the heart of the action, so you can expect invitations to fashion shows and trade fairs. If you are a good writer, you might also be asked to contribute to magazines, newspaper columns and online forums.

WHAT'S IN STORE?

It's not just designers who will need your predictions. You'll work with shop buyers to help them make decisions about what products to stock, and you may also link up with marketing teams to help them craft on-trend campaigns. Your work will appeal to fashion enthusiasts everywhere, helping them to stay up to date with all the latest styles.

Be a fashion tech designer

CREATE TECH-ENHANCED CLOTHING

Imagine a world where cutting-edge technology meets the glamour of the runway. For fashion tech designers, that's the world they live in! Working for fashion houses and tech companies, their job is to create interactive and innovative clothing using LEDs, sensors, and smart fabrics. Whether they're designing garments that respond to gestures, or accessories that respond to surroundings, fashion tech designers are creating a future where fashion is not just worn but experienced in a whole new way.

PUSHING BOUNDARIES

Fashion tech designers bring fashion shows to life in ways that were once unimaginable. Picture a model striding down the runway in a gown that changes colour with the beat of the music, or a suit that responds to the audience's applause. These incredible garments not only wow the crowd but also push the boundaries of what fashion can be, offering glimpses into the future of clothing and self-expression.

SMART SPECTACLES AND GPS JACKETS

Technology is an integral part of our daily lives, so the work of fashion tech designers couldn't be more relevant. Beyond the runway, their creations have practical applications in healthcare and fitness: think of smart watches and glasses, hi-tech fabric that regulates body temperature during exercise, and even clothing that links with digital maps to offer navigation assistance for the visually impaired.

THE FUTURE OF FASHION

Fashion tech designers need to be experts in programming and materials science, but also have an eye for design. They work closely with designers, engineers, and models; one day they may find themselves backstage of a runway show, then collaborating in a busy tech lab the next. Plus, the field is still evolving, presenting exciting opportunities for innovation in the future.

IF YOU'RE A

- word - WHIZZ...

We live in a world where communication knows no bounds and words hold the power to shape ideas, emotions, and even entire societies.

Whether you dream of becoming an author, a modern language buff or any sort of wordsmith, there are many diverse and fascinating careers you can consider.

Poetry, journalism, translating and writing stories all share a common skill: that of weaving words artfully. A good grasp of language and understanding your audience are your foundation, while confidence in your ability and creative expression will add colour to your word landscape.

REWRITE TEXTS IN DIFFERENT LANGUAGES

In a world that is more interconnected than ever before, translators play an important role in breaking down language barriers and helping people communicate across cultures. Their job is to translate one written language into another, while sticking closely to the meaning of the original text – whether that's novels, websites, legal documents, or technical manuals. Authors rely on translators to reach global audiences with their books, and businesses need their services to work across international markets.

MOTHER TONGUE

Translators generally translate into their mother tongue (their first language), making sure translations are accurate, sound natural, and capture cultural meaning well. Of course, they still need to have an excellent grasp of the original text, so fluency in both languages is essential. If you want to be a translator, it's a good idea to visit or even live in the country whose language you are translating. You should be happy to work on your own, and love immersing yourself in new cultures and languages.

THE ART OF COMPROMISE

The work of a translator goes beyond changing words from one language to another. The way we write and speak in our own language doesn't always have an exact equivalent in another – for example, everyday expressions (known as idioms) often differ across cultures. Translating is an art that requires a deep understanding of these differences and the linguistic subtleties that make each language unique.

CREATIVE LICENCE

When translating fiction or poems, the translator also needs to bring their own literary talent into play, to capture the essence of the original text. In fantasy books, for example, translators have to figure out how to recreate the names of imaginary places, spells, and even magical creatures!

BONJOUR

GUTEN TAG

HOLA

TRANSLATE SPEECH ON THE SPOT

While translators work with the written word, interpreters navigate the spoken word – translating speech from one language into another on the spot. Translators can take their time to carefully select the perfect words, while interpreters must think on their feet and respond at lightning speed. It's a linguistic live performance where the spotlight never fades!

SPECIALISED KNOWLEDGE

Professional interpreters generally have one or more qualifications under their belt, and some will also specialise in a specific field – like healthcare, law, or business. Community interpreters are needed in hospitals and clinics where healthcare providers might need to communicate with patients who speak different languages. In civil court cases involving international clients, specialist legal interpreters are hired to help lawyers and judges.

DIPLOMATIC POWER

Embassy staff and government officials also rely on interpreters to converse with their counterparts from different countries during diplomatic visits, negotiations, and important summits.

WORD WORKOUT

Often fluent in multiple languages, interpreters also possess the ability to decode body language and pick up on cultural cues, adding richness and depth to interpretation. Having to understand accents, expressions, and cultural references 'on the hoof' also makes for a seriously challenging mental workout.

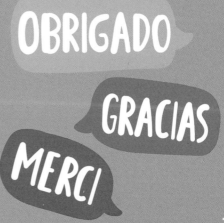

OBRIGADO

GRACIAS

MERCI

Be a screenwriter

WRITE STORIES FOR FILM AND TV

The starting point of every blockbuster film or hit TV show is a really great script. Whether that's a drama about a distant galaxy or a sitcom about a funny family, they all begin within the imagination of the screenwriter. It's their job to put those ideas on paper, transforming a blank page into a scintillating script.

WORLD BUILDING

A script is a lot more than just lines of dialogue for actors to memorise. A vivid imagination and being able to describe what you're thinking in detail is key. As a screenwriter, it's your job to craft an engaging plot, write memorable characters and create striking settings – all of which require lots of drafting and background research. Because you are effectively writing a filmed play, you will also need to write 'action lines' for the actors, which are suggestions for how they could perform the scene. These instructions also guide the director and film crew on how to translate your words from page to screen.

3, 2, 1... ACTION!

Success in scriptwriting often comes from a combination of talent, dedication, and persistence. You will want to create a strong portfolio and look for opportunities to meet people in the industry.

A big part of the job is pitching your ideas to producers, which takes confidence in speaking as well as writing.

DID YOU KNOW?

It's common for film and TV scripts to involve multiple writers. It's much easier to change something on the page than it is once it's been filmed. Different writers may be hired at different times to work on different aspects of the script. This can include the initial screenplay, rewrites, revisions, and polishing. Additionally, for TV shows, there may be a team of writers responsible for different episodes or seasons. Some scriptwriters are known as 'script doctors'. They specialise in rewriting scripts that are not working as well as they should.

Be an intelligence officer

GATHER SECRET INFO FOR NATIONAL SECURITY

Being able to speak other languages is a key skill for intelligence workers – otherwise known as spies! Their job is to gather secret information about other countries, which could be to do with politics, the military, or that country's own spying operations. By translating the information and passing it back to their own government, intelligence officers help to keep their home countries safe. The ability to speak multiple languages allows spies to carry out missions all around the world, tackling their objectives with a very low risk of detection.

BEYOND BORDERS

But it's not just about keeping a low profile – spies often need to completely conceal their identities and actually blend in as locals. This requires total fluency in the local language to avoid suspicion, gain people's trust, and piece together the bigger picture. Intelligence offers may also have to decipher coded language. Imagine intercepting an important message that's spoken entirely in code. To most, it might sound like a jumble of nonsense words. For code-cracking spies, it's a goldmine!

TOP-SECRET TECH

Intelligence officers are tech-savvy too, often taking advantage of the latest technology to eavesdrop on conversations without being detected – for example, by using wiretapping devices to listen in on telephone calls. This is known as electronic eavesdropping.

I SPY WITH MY LITTLE EYE

Due to the classified nature of this role, the day-to-day tasks of a spy are mostly a mystery! But if you're good under pressure and can think on your feet, you just might have what it takes to get the job and find out more...

135

Be a social media strategist

DEVELOP DIGITAL CONTENT FOR BUSINESSES

With over half of the world's population now using social media platforms, their reach is undeniable. A well-crafted social post can go viral in seconds and help to shape public opinion, showing how social media is not just a way to connect with others – it can also be a powerful business tool. That's why companies hire social media strategists to manage their social media accounts and create original content. It's a career that suits those who like creating content, have a strong understanding of how people behave online, and have awareness of the latest trends.

SOCIAL SKILLS

Social media strategists plan and schedule content in advance – but it's not just about a few well-timed posts. You'll need to know how each social platform works, who uses them, and how to create dynamic content that will grab your audience's attention. The ability to multitask is a must, as you'll be responsible for managing multiple social media accounts.

POSTING PLAN

As a social media strategist, you'll create a timetable for regular posting, decide on which videos or photos to use for each platform, write witty captions with trending hashtags, and respond to comments from customers. You'll also use analytics tools to report on your success at the end of the campaign.

GO VIRAL

In 2020, footballer Marcus Rashford campaigned via social media for vulnerable children in the UK to continue to receive free meals over the summer holidays. His campaign received so much support that the UK government was persuaded to change its plans. This goes to show how social media can bring about real-world change.

SUBSCRIBE

Be an investigative journalist

RESEARCH AND WRITE SERIOUS NEWS STORIES

In the world of journalism, the written word wields a unique power to tell important stories, uncover hidden truths, and change people's minds. Investigative journalists research and write about serious topics, like political events or current affairs, and they typically work for newspapers, magazines, and TV stations. If you are driven by curiosity and have a flair for finding out the truth, a career in investigative journalism promises to be an exciting journey.

FACT FINDERS

Investigative journalists don't just record events as they happen; they write detailed accounts of complex issues and put the spotlight on major stories. They spend a lot of time researching their topic and fact-checking sources and will reach out to subject experts to arrange interviews. Once they have all the information they need, it's time to write the story – using proper grammar, spelling, and style – before sending it out into the world.

TRUTH TELLERS

An aspiring investigative journalist will need to be determined, with an eye for detail and the courage to face difficult truths head-on. A knack for research and a tenacious, curious mind will help, especially if you are particularly keen on putting pen to paper to express your findings.

CHANGE MAKERS

The power of revealing the truth through the written word is immense. Research shows that stories about real people have a bigger influence on government leaders than just showing them numbers and facts. That's why working as an investigative journalist, and helping to bring about change, can be so incredibly rewarding.

RECORD YOUR OWN AUDIO PROGRAMME

Although many jobs involve spending lots of time in front of screens, a listening revolution is also happening through our headphones – it's called podcasting. People all around the world tune into podcasts weekly for their dose of gripping crime mysteries, insightful political debates, or deep dives into their favourite hobbies. Nowadays, there is truly a podcast for everything.

SOUND EFFECT

The spoken word is the only medium used in podcasting, with no need for visuals. Podcasts get their personality through different voices, perspectives, and stories – making language not just a tool, but the heart of the experience. Many listeners feel a personal connection with podcast hosts, often referring to them as friends or mentors. With smart speakers and hands-free technology now part of our everyday lives, podcasting is an easy way to connect with any audience.

GET CREATIVE

Podcasting isn't just about speaking – it's a great way to express your creativity. From storytelling, comedy, opinion pieces, and everything in between, podcasts are an opportunity for you to explore the things that interest you.

PRESS PLAY

Starting a podcast is fairly easy and cheap. With basic recording equipment and access to the internet – through a tablet or smartphone – virtually anyone can create and publish their own podcast. The main decision to make is what you want your theme or topic to be!

Be a children's book author

WRITE STORIES FOR YOUNG READERS

Children's book authors play an important role in encouraging a love of reading that stretches beyond childhood. Through their words, they don't just provide entertainment; they nurture young minds, helping to improve critical thinking and social skills. It's a job that stands the test of time – as long as young readers yearn for stories that spark their imaginations, the role of the children's author remains invaluable.

KNOW YOUR AUDIENCE

Children are often a discerning audience: they pay great attention to details in stories and want both a sense of the familiar but also surprise and delight in the characters and situations they encounter. As a writer, you need to step into the shoes of your young reader, understand their dreams, fears, joys, and what they find funny.

RESPECT YOUR READERSHIP

One of the myths about children's writing is that you need to use simple language and 'childish' storylines. You do need to pitch your language right, but the true art is handling sometimes difficult themes in a way that is accessible, engaging, and respectful of a young reader's intelligence and experience. This balance will keep your readers challenged, inspired and eager for more.

FICTION AND FACT

While fiction feeds the imagination, non-fiction improves our understanding of the real world. The landscape of children's literature isn't limited to fantastical stories – we need books that deal with facts to educate, inspire, and ignite curiosity about science, art, history, nature... and even extraordinary real-world jobs!

WHY DID YOU CHOOSE YOUR JOB?

I have always been passionate about books. Stories transport us to different times, different places, different worlds. When you read, you're wandering through the realms of someone else's imagination – what an amazing way to connect with other people's thoughts! Reading is the closest thing we have to time travel. And as a writer, I can create that magic for readers.

HOW DID YOU GET INTO YOUR JOB?

Lots of practice! I wrote in my spare time. In diaries, notebooks, sketchbooks. I loved using words to express how I saw the world around me, what I thought. I joined writing groups.

I met my now editor while I was running a history workshop about Black Georgians in London. She had the idea to create a mystery series about the writer Ignatius Sancho and invited me to write a novel – and *The Lizzie and Belle Mysteries* grew from there!

HOW LONG HAVE YOU BEEN DOING IT FOR?

I've been a professional writer for three years, but I've been writing since I was a child. I used to be a school teacher, which I loved. Now I work in a university and I get to teach Creative Writing to emerging writers, as well as doing my own research and writing. It feels like the perfect job!

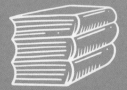

"Reading is the closest thing we have to time travel. And as a writer, I can create that magic for readers."

WHAT QUALIFICATIONS AND EXPERIENCE DID YOU NEED TO DO THE JOB?

Strictly speaking, you don't need particular qualifications to be a writer. But you do have to love reading and writing. Think about the books that you love, that draw you in. What is it about them that is special? Nurture your own ideas. Write as often as you can and read your work aloud, to hear how it sounds. Then be prepared to edit and change and improve it until it sounds just the way you want it to.

WHAT IS A SURPRISING FACT ABOUT YOUR JOB?

To research my books I go on trips: I walk the city, I visit museums and galleries, I listen to music. Walking in the places and spaces that my characters might have walked in is a great source of inspiration to me!

WHAT ARE THE HIGHLIGHTS OF YOUR JOB?

The highlight is that I get to spend time creating worlds and people in my imagination, then bring them to life on the page. Holding your own book in your hands is a wonderful feeling. I also love going into schools and hearing directly from readers about the books.

As with any worthwhile endeavour, the work can be difficult at times. You might spend hours trying to 'solve' a problem in the story. It can be frustrating. But the joy of having a lightbulb moment in the middle of the night, or on a walk, or on the bus, is its own reward!

Joanna signing copies of Drama and Danger from *The Lizzie and Belle Mysteries* series

CREATE YOUR OWN LANGUAGES

Do you ever make up your own language to swap secrets with your friends? If so, a career as a conlanger is calling you! Conlangers, short for 'constructed language creators', are people who specialise in creating imaginary languages, known as conlangs, from scratch. Conlangs are used to add a sense of reality to fictional worlds in films, TV shows, and video games.

A WAY WITH WORDS

A conlanger is both a linguist and an artist, combining technical linguistic knowledge with creative imagination. The conlanger's work contributes depth and authenticity to storytelling. Conlangs aren't just random strings of sounds; they have complex grammatical rules and detailed vocabulary that mirror real languages.

IT'S ALL ELVISH TO ME

Did you know that J.R.R. Tolkien invented the languages Elvish and Dwarvish for his books? He fully integrated his conlangs into the cultures of his fictional people, tying them to the histories, mythologies, and societies of Middle-earth.

GET IT DOWN

Documenting your invented language is crucial for communicating it to others. Conlangers create grammar guides and dictionaries to ensure the language is used consistently over time. If their conlangs are used in film and TV, they may also work with actors to teach them the right pronunciation.

Be a slam poet

PERFORM POETRY FOR AN AUDIENCE

A slam poet is a creative writer and performer who uses words to express ideas and connect with an audience in a meaningful way. They take part in poetry competitions, or 'slams', where they perform in front of an audience and a panel of judges. The judges assign scores based on the quality of the poems, the performance, and the audience's reaction. The poets usually have a strict time limit to perform their piece, often around three minutes – making these rather exciting events!

SLAM DUNK

Slam poetry is a form of creative expression that celebrates the spoken word and the art of performance. As well as performing, some slam poets make a living by publishing their work in anthologies or online.

EXPRESS YOURSELF

Slam poetry covers a wide range of topics, including social issues, identity, love, politics, and lots more. Diversity is key – it's a great platform for voices from different backgrounds to be heard and respected. Poets often use their performances to convey intense feelings, connecting with the audience on an emotional level. Poets are encouraged to share their authentic experiences and perspectives, often drawing from their own lives.

PUT YOUR FINGERS TOGETHER

Slam poets often engage with the audience during their performances to create a dynamic atmosphere. They encourage call-and-response interactions, cheers, and 'snaps' – a form of applause where the audience snap their fingers.

Published by Collins
An imprint of HarperCollins Publishers
Westerhill Road
Bishopbriggs
Glasgow
G64 2QT

HarperCollins Publishers
Macken House, 39/40 Mayor Street Upper, Dublin 1, D01 C9W8, Ireland

collins.co.uk

First published 2024

Text © Katherine Mengardon 2024
Cover and chapter opener illustrations by Rachael Horner
Stock images © Shutterstock.com

Publisher: Beth Ralston
Project leader: Rachel Allegro
Design: Rachael Horner, Gordon MacGilp, Kevin Robbins and James Hunter
Cover: Rachael Horner
Production: Ilaria Rovera

A catalogue record for this book is available from the British Library.

ISBN: 9780008653712

Printed in India by Replika Press Pvt. Ltd.

10 9 8 7 6 5 4 3 2 1

I never knew what I wanted to do when I grew up, because I had no idea what was
possible. Chance meetings with amazing artists, scientists, wordsmiths, people in
sports, crafts, commerce and many more showed me there is indeed a space and a
need for what we love. A huge thank you and respect to all of you. With love to my
heart family of humans and felines across the world. – Katherine Mengardon